What people are sa:

Resetting Our Future:

What If Solving the Climate Crisis Is Simple?

Too often we encounter efforts to dismiss climate change as a "wicked" (that is, unsolvable) problem. But nothing could be more wicked than such unhelpful framing. As Tom Bowman explains in this inspiring, concise primer on climate action, we have the ability to surmount this mentality if we simply make the commitment to not just try but do.

Michael Mann, Distinguished Professor, Penn State University and author of *The New Climate War: The Fight to Take Back Our Planet*

As California's top official charged with developing plans to stop climate change, I am constantly told that the science and economics of global warming are too complicated for all but a small technical elite to figure out solutions. Tom Bowman turns that picture on its head and then empowers small businesses and ordinary citizens to make it happen.

Mary Nichols, Chair, California Air Resources Board

The premise of this book is crucial: though climate change is a complicated problem, the most important solution is very clear. We have to stop burning fossil fuels, and we have to do it fast. Stated that way, we can get to work.

Bill McKibben, author of *Falter: Has the Human Game Begun to Play Itself Out?*

Tom Bowman is one of the most brilliant solutions strategists of our time. I nominated him to write this book because I wanted to study his thoughts about the way forward. I'm glad I did.
Edward Maibach, Director, George Mason University Center for Climate Change Communication

This stimulating and optimistic book explores a profound truth about the climate change challenge. Framing it as inevitable catastrophe leads only to despair but focusing on simple goals and achievable solutions is the key to real success.
Richard C. J. Somerville, Distinguished Professor Emeritus, Scripps Institution of Oceanography, University of California, San Diego

Drawing on a nuanced understanding of human behavior, design thinking, and experience driving organizational change, Bowman cuts through the Gordian Knot of climate change with simple, straightforward, and practical solutions. A very useful guide to anyone seeking to make a difference.
Anthony Leiserowitz, Director, Yale Program on Climate Change Communication

Tom Bowman identifies the strategic collaborations needed to meet the climate challenge, their transformational potential for the communities and scientists involved, and the feelings of personal satisfaction and collective empowerment that will sustain them.
Baruch Fischhoff, Howard Heinz Professor, Institute for Policy and Strategy, Carnegie Mellon University

Simple solutions to complex problems need not be populist. Tom's solutions to climate are exactly what's needed to regain engagement on this defining challenge of our generation.
Per Espen Stoknes, Director, Centre for Sustainability and

Energy, Norwegian Business School and author of *Tomorrow's Economy*

Tom Bowman offers visionary solutions to vexing global challenges. He offers common sense approaches for the soft-landing civilization needs. We owe it to future generations to offer viable roadmaps.

Joel Solomon, co-founder of Renewal Funds and author of *The Clean Money Revolution*

Tom Bowman makes a compelling case to shift the paradigm from climate change to climate action. This book is an excellent opportunity for everyone to learn more about a better idea for communicating climate change. Tom puts the issue squarely on us, not them.

Sam Geil, Founder, International Green Industry Hall of Fame

RESETTING OUR FUTURE

What If Solving the Climate Crisis Is Simple?

Resetting Our Future

What If Solving the Climate Crisis Is Simple?

Tom Bowman

CHANGEMAKERS
BOOKS

Winchester, UK
Washington, USA

JOHN HUNT PUBLISHING

First published by Changemakers Books, 2020
Changemakers Books is an imprint of John Hunt Publishing Ltd., No. 3 East Street,
Alresford, Hampshire SO24 9EE, UK
office@jhpbooks.com
www.johnhuntpublishing.com
www.changemakers-books.com

For distributor details and how to order please visit the 'Ordering' section on our website.

A CIP catalogue record for this book is available from the British Library.

Design: Stuart Davies

Printed and bound by CPI Group (UK) Ltd, Croydon, CR0 4YY
Printed in North America by CPI GPS partners

We operate a distinctive and ethical publishing philosophy in
all areas of our business, from our global network of authors to
production and worldwide distribution.

Contents

The *Resetting Our Future* Series

At this critical moment of history, with a pandemic raging, we have the rare opportunity for a Great Reset – to choose a different future. This series provides a platform for pragmatic thought leaders to share their vision for change based on their deep expertise. For communities and nations struggling to cope with the crisis, these books will provide a burst of hope and energy to help us take the first difficult steps towards a better future.
– Tim Ward, publisher, Changemakers Books

What if Solving the Climate Crisis Is Simple?
Tom Bowman, President of Bowman Change, Inc., and Writing Team Lead for the U.S. ACE National Strategic Planning Framework

Zero Waste Living, the 80/20 Way
The Busy Person's Guide to a Lighter Footprint
Stephanie Miller, Founder of Zero Waste in DC, and former Director, IFC Climate Business Department.

A Chicken Can't Lay a Duck Egg
How COVID-19 can Solve the Climate Crisis
Graeme Maxton, (former Secretary-General of the Club of Rome), and Bernice Maxton-Lee (former Director, Jane Goodall Institute)

A Global Playbook for the Next Pandemic
Anne Kabagambe, World Bank Executive Director

We Should have Seen it Coming
How Foresight can Prepare us for the Next Crisis
Bart Édes, North American Representative, Asian Development Bank

Impact ED
A Roadmap for Restoring Jobs & Rebuilding the Economy
Rebecca Corbin (President, National Association of Community
College Entrepreneurship), Andrew Gold and Mary-Beth Kerly
(both business faculty, Hillsborough Community College).

Power Switch
How Activists can win the Fight Against Extreme Inequality
Paul O'Brien, VP, Policy and Advocacy, Oxfam America

Creating a Paradigm Shift to Achieve the Global SDGs
A SMART Futures Mindset for a Sustainable World.
Dr. Claire Nelson, Chief Visionary Officer and Lead Futurist,
The Futures Forum

Reconstructing Blackness
Rev. Charles Howard, Chaplin, University of
Pennsylvania, Philadelphia.

Cut Super Climate Pollutants, Now!
The Ozone Treaty's Urgent Lessons for Speeding up Climate Action
Alan Miller (former World Bank representative for global
climate negotiations) and Durwood Zaelke, (President, The
Institute for Governance & Sustainable Development, and
co-director, The Program on Governance for Sustainable
Development at UC Santa Barbara)

www.ResettingOurFuture.com

Previous Books by Tom Bowman

The Green Edge

ISBN-10: 0991570308
ISBN-13: 978-0991570300

For Sam and Lee
May we create a future that inspires you.

Foreword

by Thomas Lovejoy

The Pandemic has changed our world. Lives have been lost. Livelihoods as well. Far too many face urgent problems of health and economic security, but almost all of us are reinventing our lives in one way or another. Meeting the immediate needs of the less fortunate is obviously a priority, and a big one. But beyond those compassionate imperatives, there is also tremendous opportunity for what some people are calling a "Great Reset." This series of books, *Resetting Our Future*, is designed to provide pragmatic visionary ideas and stimulate a fundamental rethink of the future of humanity, nature and the economy.

I find myself thinking about my parents, who had lived through the Second World War and the Great Depression, and am still impressed by the sense of frugality they had attained. When packages arrived in the mail, my father would save the paper and string; he did it so systematically I don't recall our ever having to buy string. Our diets were more careful: whether it could be afforded or not, beef was restricted to once a week. When aluminum foil – the great boon to the kitchen – appeared, we used and washed it repeatedly until it fell apart. Bottles, whether coca cola or milk, were recycled.

Waste was consciously avoided. My childhood task was to put out the trash; what goes out of my backdoor today is an unnecessary multiple of that. At least some of it now goes to recycling but a lot more should surely be possible.

There was also a widespread sense of service to a larger community. Military service was required of all. But there was also the Civilian Conservation Corps, which had provided jobs and repaired the ecological destruction that had generated the Dust Bowl. The Kennedy administration introduced the Peace

Corps and the President's phrase "Ask not what your country can do for you but what you can do for your country" still resonates in our minds.

There had been antecedents, but in the 1970s there was a global awakening about a growing environmental crisis. In 1972, The United Nations held its first conference on the environment at Stockholm. Most of the modern US institutions and laws about environment were established under moderate Republican administrations (Nixon and Ford). Environment was seen not just as appealing to "greenies" but also as a thoughtful conservative's issue. The largest meeting of Heads of State in history, The Earth Summit, took place in Rio de Janeiro in 1992 and three international conventions -- climate change, biodiversity (on which I was consulted) and desertification -- came into existence.

But three things changed. First, there now are three times as many people alive today as when I was born and each new person deserves a minimum quality of life. Second, the sense of frugality was succeeded by a growing appetite for affluence and an overall attitude of entitlement. And third, conservative political advisors found advantage in demonizing the environment as comity vanished from the political dialogue.

Insufficient progress has brought humanity and the environment to a crisis state. The CO_2 level in the atmosphere at 415 ppm (parts per million) is way beyond a non-disruptive level around 350 ppm. (The pre-industrial level was 280 ppm.)

Human impacts on nature and biodiversity are not just confined to climate change. Those impacts will not produce just a long slide of continuous degradation. The Pandemic is a direct result of intrusion upon, and destruction of, nature as well as wild-animal trade and markets. The scientific body of the UN Convention on Biological Diversity warned in 2020 that we could lose a million species unless there are major changes in human interactions with nature.

We still can turn those situations around. Ecosystem restoration at scale could pull carbon back out of the atmosphere for a soft landing at 1.5 degrees of warming (at 350 ppm), hand in hand with a rapid halt in production and use of fossil fuels. The Amazon tipping point where its hydrological cycle would fail to provide enough rain to maintain the forest in southern and Eastern Amazonia can be solved with major reforestation. The oceans' biology is struggling with increasing acidity, warming and ubiquitous pollution with plastics: addressing climate change can lower the first two and efforts to remove plastics from our waste stream can improve the latter.

Indisputably, we need a major reset in our economies, what we produce, and what we consume. We exist on an amazing living planet, with a biological profusion that can provide humanity a cornucopia of benefits—and more that science has yet to reveal—and all of it is automatically recyclable because nature is very good at that. Scientists have determined that we can, in fact, feed all the people on the planet, and the couple billion more who may come, by a combination of selective improvements of productivity, eliminating food waste and altering our diets (which our doctors have been advising us to do anyway).

The *Resetting Our Future* series is intended to help people think about various ways of economic and social rebuilding that will support humanity for the long term. There is no single way to do this and there is plenty of room for creativity in the process, but nature with its capacity for recovery and for recycling can provide us with much inspiration, including ways beyond our current ability to imagine.

Ecosystems do recover from shocks, but the bigger the shock, the more complicated recovery can be. At the end of the Cretaceous period (66 million years ago) a gigantic meteor slammed into the Caribbean near the Yucatan and threw up so much dust and debris into the atmosphere that much of biodiversity perished. It was *sayonara* for the dinosaurs; their only surviving close relatives were precursors to modern day birds. It certainly was not a good time for life on Earth.

The clear lesson of the pandemic is that it makes no sense to generate a global crisis and then hope for a miracle. We are lucky to have the pandemic help us reset our relation to the Living Planet as a whole. We already have building blocks like the United Nations Sustainable Development Goals and various environmental Conventions to help us think through more effective goals and targets. The imperative is to rebuild with humility and imagination, while always conscious of the health of the living planet on which we have the joy and privilege to exist.

Dr. Thomas E. Lovejoy is Professor of Environmental Science and Policy at George Mason University and a Senior Fellow at the United Nations Foundation. A world-renowned conservation biologist, Dr. Lovejoy introduced the term "biological diversity" to the scientific community.

Acknowledgements

I owe many people a great debt of thanks for making this book and my work on the climate crisis possible. Most importantly, thanks to my wife, Tina, for her encouragement, patience and support over more than two decades.

A publisher who is tuned in to a book's ideas yet retains a reader's perspective becomes an invaluable creative partner. Special thanks to Timothy Ward of Changemaker Books. Thanks, also, to the other authors in the *Resetting Our Future* book series; their collective wisdom and dedication are inspiring.

Speaking of creative partners, special thanks to Ed Hackley, my lifelong collaborator, who presses relentlessly for greater clarity, elegance and refreshing surprise.

I am indebted to the mentors in science, especially climate science, who generously taught me about the global crises we face and, just as importantly, how to interpret scientific information: Bruce Alberts, Richard Alley, Ilan Chabay, Michael Mann, Douglas McCauley, Michael Osterholm, Naomi Oreskes, Veerabhadran Ramanathan, Cynthia Rosenzweig, Erika Schugart, Peter Schultz, Richard Somerville, Michael Wallace, Debbie Zmarzly, and others. Thanks, as well, to the institutional leaders who created some of these valuable relationships, including Patrice Legro, Nigella Hillgarth, Daniel Koshland and Jerry Schubel.

It was Shinzen Young who, in response to an urgent question, said, "Sure, I have lots of ideas. I just don't believe them." Those words stuck. Decades later, I owe great thanks to the mentors in the social sciences who taught me how to apply systematic evidence about human psychology to creative projects and campaigns. Thanks to Baruch Fischhoff, Rob Gould, Jon Krosnick, Anthony Leiserowitz, Edward Maibach, Connie Roser-Renouf and Yasuyuki Owada.

Thanks to the leaders in government who have shown

me how the world of policymaking and, especially, policy implementation can improve our lives, especially Susan Callery, David Herring, Parvin Kassaie, Louisa Koch and Frank Niepold.

Special thanks to Mary Nichols and the staff of the California Air Resources Board for creating a small business recognition program that opened a door for me to the diversity of leaders who have committed their businesses to reducing global warming. And thanks to Gary Erickson for demonstrating what inspired and authentic entrepreneurship looks like. I am also indebted to the staff of Bowman Design Group for their commitment to an ambitious decarbonization plan: Jim Cain, Katerina Gabbro, Samantha Gammell, Alex Gjonovich, Lee Harrington, Jake Huttner, Teri Metcalf, Gail Mutke, Erin Nichols and Sora Cin.

So many other collaborators, colleagues, friends and supporters share the important work of climate empowerment. A few who have been influential are Ruben Aronin, Jeff Baker, Anthony Bigio, David Blockstein, Alex Bozmoski, Kateri Callahan, Ann Carpenter, Renee Chu-Jacoby, Isates Cintron-Rodriguez, Jeff Chase, Haley Crim, Timothy Damon, Cyane Dandridge, Andrew Dessler, Simon Donner, Mike Ellis, Ignacio Fernandez, Susan Frank, Howard Frumkin, Michael Gallagher, Stephen Gardiner, Roland Geiger, Sam Geil, Kate Gordon, Stephen Groner, Jay Gulledge, Elysa Hammond, Michael Hanemann, Heidi Harmon, Charles Harris, Catherine Hart, Susan Joy Hassol, Wendy James, Tim Juliani, Kat Janowicz, Laura Kovary, Jen Kretser, Tamara Ledley, David Lustick, Ingrid Martin, Wade Martin, Miranda Massie, Jeff Nesbit, Mark McCaffrey, Richard McCaskill, Bill McKibben, Deb Morrison, Duane Muller, Jonathan Parfrey, William Patzert, Jay Penev, Cara Pike, Kristen Poppleton, Sassan Rahimzadeh, Andrew Revkin, Clay Sandidge, Arno Scharl, KoAnn Skrzyniarz, David Sobel, William Solecki, Joel Solomon, Per Espen Stoknes, Tom Steyer, Denise Taschereau, Marcia Tolentino, Dagny Scott, Billy Spitzer, Stella Ursua, Cynthia Vernon, Bud Ward, Bill Weihl, Laura Weiland, Jodine West, Andrew Winston and Gary Yohe.

Chapter One

Are We Too Late to Solve the Climate Crisis?

It is easy to think we have already failed. But thoughts are not reality. They are just mental pictures, interpretations and stories about our circumstances that we tell ourselves and come to believe. The things we believe affect our choices, of course, but they are not monolithic, nor are they set in stone. We can test them, and, if we find our thoughts wanting, we can change them. People change their minds all the time.

The question of whether we are too late to solve the climate crisis has a certain dramatic flair. It sounds cinematic, and it captures a sense of anxiety that makes this moment in time feel supercharged. It also creates a temptation to feel hopeless. That temptation gets reinforced day after day by news stories, scientific reports, documentaries, topical books and the sales pitches from activist organizations. You can probably recite the litany of woes by heart. It goes something like this: global temperatures break records almost every year. Carbon pollution in the atmosphere has never been higher and continues to rise. The financial costs of climate-related disasters are escalating, and the human costs of forced migration, sickness and death continue to mount.

These are facts, of course, but they are not conclusions, and this is a crucial distinction. Although the trend leans toward increased global warming, new solutions are being implemented all over the world. In fact, a second trend is emerging in favor of tackling the climate crisis. Nothing has actually been decided in a literal sense.

Even in the United States, where the federal government ping-pongs between action and inaction, the frustrating instability of climate policy demonstrates just how fluid the situation really is. This bit of history is probably familiar as well: unable to pass a climate bill, the Obama administration relied on executive authority to press ahead with the landmark Paris Agreement and stricter limits on pollution from vehicles and coal-fired powerplants. The Trump administration, in turn, used executive authority to reverse course, rolling back clean air and clean water rules, and announcing its intention to leave the Paris Agreement. The people who support each side tend to inhabit their chosen news bubbles where wildly different interpretations of the issues reinforce but rarely question their worldviews.

All the while, time flies by. According to an influential 2018 Special Report by the Intergovernmental Panel on Climate Change (IPCC) the goal of limiting warming substantially below 2°C looks ever more elusive.[1] Limiting warming to 1.5°C might actually require extracting carbon dioxide from the atmosphere and placing it in long-term storage. With each passing year, bolder actions and commitments become necessary. Industrialized nations need to decarbonize rapidly while developing nations try to avoid becoming reliant on fossils fuels.

On top of all this, the COVID-19 pandemic and the resulting unemployment and financial upheaval, plus the wrenching exposure of long-standing police violence and racial injustice in the United States add to a heightened sense of compounding urgency. Tragedy and grief have invaded our lives, and we simply cannot return to what we knew before we got to this point.

These observations are so familiar that they probably read like clichés. They express the accepted wisdom in a nation that seems to be paralyzed. And people are not very optimistic about the future. Roughly half of the public in the U.S. thinks global warming could be reduced, but only six percent think humanity will succeed in doing so.[2] They are not alone. In 2019, an international survey found widespread pessimism in developed nations that we will be better off in five years' time. The overwhelming majority of people, in fact, do not think "the system" is working for them.[3]

That's the news. It is probably as familiar as an old pair of shoes, but is it a complete and accurate picture of where we stand? More importantly, is this where we want to be? If not, is there a way out? I think there is.

In their book about how people and organizations make decisions, Chip and Dan Heath observe that "humanity does not have a particularly impressive track record."[4] We humans tend to give too much weight to the information that is right in front of our eyes instead of broadening the view to consider more data. The ways in which we frame problems are often too narrow. We collect and prioritize new information that confirms our existing beliefs, while rejecting or downplaying information that challenges those beliefs. We are prone to rush toward judgments based on short-term emotions. When we make decisions, we have a tendency to be overconfident about how the future will unfold, which leads us to resist adjusting our course.

Tendencies such as these suggest that the ways in which we look at problems are often flawed. Humanity comes by its flaws honestly, though, or at least by way of evolution. Evolution favors efficiency, and our brains are fine-tuned to simplify our lives by building and reusing familiar scripts. In other words, we are predisposed to trust tried and true perceptions, even if they are wrong.

Everyday Survival is the second of three books in which Laurence Gonzales explores the connections between evolution, psychology and catastrophe. Among many extraordinary stories, he describes a tragedy that occurred when a tsunami in the Indian Ocean struck the coast of Thailand on December 26, 2004. He sees the unfortunate events that followed as a conflict between well-worn behavioral scripts and the harsh reality of an unfamiliar event.

One of the most haunting videos shows people on the beach at Panang, milling about, walking casually, or standing in relaxed attitudes, hands on hips, as the great wave approaches in the background. They seem completely unaware. One of them is obviously recording the video. They all see the wave but do not move away. When the wave reaches them at last, they laugh as it gathers around their feet and ankles and begins to rise. Only when the wave knocks them off their feet and starts to sweep them away do they scream, as they comprehend the grave miscalculation they've made.

Not everyone had an opportunity to survive. ...many who could have escaped did not, because nothing in their experience had prepared them for an event that, in geologic time, happens routinely where the land meets the sea.[5]

Then comes a crucial observation about human nature:

Educated and sophisticated as those people may have been, their mental models and behavioral scripts were useless when their environment underwent a completely predictable change. They had created a stable mental model of their world and an indelible script for what they were doing. They were on vacation in the benign sunshine of a happy beach. Only at the last, as they were knocked over, did the wave sweep away that model and rewrite that script, in many cases too late to do them any good in the future.[6]

This is precisely what we want to avoid as we confront the climate crisis. Do you see the challenge? The focal point needs to move away from the climate system itself and into our own minds, where our perceptions, the accepted wisdom, and our lack of confidence are getting us into trouble.

Perceptions feed powerful and durable scripts until they are disrupted. Fortunately, when something shakes people free, surprising opportunities await. This happened in 1954, for example, when Roger Bannister broke an impossible-looking barrier by running the first sub-four-minute mile. Fifty years later, the record was more than sixteen seconds faster. Gonzales notes, "Humans had not evolved into gazelles in those few years. What changed were the mental models and scripts of the runners."[7]

He concludes that, "Mental models make our world, but they also shape and constrain the possible."[8] It stands to reason, then, that there might be more to the climate story than meets the eye. Is there more to see? If so, how can we see it?

The best advice I ever received on this score came from an art professor. He suggested that when nothing seems to be working, hang the troublesome picture upside down and then go home. That way, you will surely to see it differently when you come back. I made good use of this advice when I owned a design agency, and I eventually used it to develop an analogous strategy for rethinking other types of problems as well.

Here is the basic idea: when a problem seems insoluble, no matter how many different approaches you try, ask yourself if every failed solution has an assumption, a premise, or a requirement in common. The more rock solid and important that assumption or requirement seems, the better. When you find it, try setting it aside and see what happens. In my experience, setting aside the most crucial, fundamental premise you can find has a way of unraveling even the most complex and frustrating challenges. The mental routines get disrupted and new possibilities present themselves. Given the high stakes involved in the climate crisis, we should give this a try.

We have plenty to work with. To many of us, the climate crisis looks like a thicket of entwined and interacting problems involving complex and sprawling systems. Pulling on any one thread can quickly entangle you in many others: energy generation and distribution, buildings and urban planning, transportation systems that serve hometowns and span the world, global supply chains, investments and financial markets, corporate governance, civic governance, international development and international aid, consumer behavior, waste management, national and global security, education, environmental justice and human rights, ecosystem resilience and so much more. Carving the puzzle into smaller pieces helps to a degree, but at some point, each part inevitably pulls on other parts too.

As a result, global warming strikes a lot of people as a so-called "wicked problem." Wicked problem is a term given to challenges that are essentially too complex to solve. In grappling with a wicked problem, the requirements and essential information might be hard to identify, impossible to get or constantly changing. The problem itself might defy any clear definition. Solving the wicked problem that you can see might create other problems that you cannot see, which makes the pursuit of solutions never ending. The best outcome might be that people work very hard, do the best they can and, inevitably, end up taking some lumps anyway. A great many public presentations about global warming, in fact, conclude with heartfelt admonitions that we must prevent catastrophe by somehow mustering the political and personal willpower to do the best we can against seemingly insurmountable odds.

More than a decade ago, in response to this type of call to action, a political psychologist at Stanford University named Jon Krosnick pointed out that it is awfully difficult to generate public enthusiasm for expensive and inconvenient halfway measures that will not solve the problem.[9] The whole idea seems self-defeating, and most people know from experience that willpower is a finite resource. We get tired. We get distracted. And we conclude that if the problem cannot be solved it is not worth our attention anyway.

Unfortunately, accepting such a discouraging outlook leaves people feeling powerless and vulnerable to another type of pressure as well. This pressure comes from a long-term, sophisticated and well-financed campaign by fossil fuel companies and ideological libertarians to mislead people about the climate crisis and dissuade them from taking action.[10] The campaign makes use of think tanks that publish seemingly credible but misleading pseudo-science, lobbyists and organizations that draft sample legislation in their favor, and messengers who voice opinions that certain media outlets will always amplify and repeat. The people behind this campaign know how to reinforce discouraging mental models. They also know that sowing doubt and stoking resentment are much easier than building trust and encouraging thoughtful deliberation.

With all this going on, then, why not ignore climate change and worry about something else instead? Why not trust the weather if it looks good today? If we happen to be pushing on nature a little bit, surely it will compensate and snap back to normal like it always has in the past. After all, people have a pandemic, their financial wellbeing and the education of their children to cope with, so there is plenty to worry about already.

Human psychology is, in fact, tuned to give top priority to immediate, tangible threats such as these. The COVID-19 crisis of 2020 showed us some of the things people and societies are capable of doing in response. With remarkable speed, people changed their behavior in ways that would have seemed unthinkable only a few months earlier. In huge numbers, people sacrificed their jobs and businesses in order to avoid infection and "flatten the curve." Governments quickly shifted trillions of dollars to provide relief. In the United States, however, people saw the curve flattening and made the mistake of paying too much attention to the good news. Like the people who stood on the beach in Panang and watched the tsunami wave approach, people in the United States shut their ears to the warnings of science and health experts and reverted to the familiar scripts that said life can always return to normal. Only when the wave of new infections and deaths began their sharp rise and overtopped the capacity of many hospitals did people begin to question their assumptions.

Fortunately, public concern about the climate crisis is growing too. As of 2020, a significant majority of Americans (57%) say they are "alarmed" or "concerned" about global warming.[11] These numbers have never been higher. Just two years earlier, forty percent already said they had experienced the effects of global warming personally and that the changing climate is already harming the nation.[12]

All of which begs the question: is the idea that climate change is a wicked problem actually helpful?

For some professionals, analyzing and adjusting entangled and interacting systems is essential, but does this apply to everyone? Does it apply to you? A description of the climate crisis that involves a tangle of large-scale systems might be accurate from a certain top-down point of view, but it is a mental model of the situation, which means that it is only one possible interpretation. Is this interpretation a useful way to frame the search for solutions? Does it describe the processes by which social change actually occurs? More importantly, does it help you, and everyone you know, feel empowered and engaged?

What if the "wicked problem" is that singular premise that makes people lose hope? This notion of an insoluble entanglement is deeply entrenched in our thinking. We take it for granted. This makes the idea a good candidate to try setting aside. If abandoning such a fundamental understanding strikes you as intellectually irresponsible, consider this: the centrality of this idea is the key feature that makes the thought experiment worthwhile. If we want to get a different perspective on the problem, it makes sense to take our most strongly held assumptions off the table.

Consider this as well: people tend to defend the status quo, even when the status quo is harmful and dispiriting. Defending the status quo is another inherent tendency in human psychology. Relatively few people choose behaviors or ideas that they think will be more beneficial if making the change is inconvenient or expensive. Think about how often you make the effort to opt out of something or change your basic point of view. People rarely opt out unless they feel extremely motivated to do so. There is a silver lining, of course, which is that when the status quo changes people adapt quickly and then defend the new norm. We are, in a sense, creatures of habit in our behaviors, thoughts and beliefs.[13]

So, on a provisional basis at least, let us suppose that our most basic premise about the climate crisis is all wrong. What will we discover if we set it aside? This seems like a good time to hang our mental picture of global warming upside down and take a fresh look. Perhaps this dark moment in history will turn out to be a rare moment of opportunity.

Chapter 2

Hang the Climate Crisis Upside Down

Suppose, at least for a moment, that the climate crisis is not a wicked problem after all. Suppose it is simple, like the Gordian Knot. It looks complex, but we can cut through it with a single stroke. If human activities are causing the climate system to warm, as the scientific community has concluded,[1] it stands to reason that changing human behavior will stop the warming. Suppose we really believed this. What would we do differently? The answer is very simple: we would just stop burning fossil fuels.

We also want to make our communities more resilient to the changes that can no longer be avoided, of course, and also address other reasons why greenhouse gases are building up in the atmosphere. These include deforestation, farming practices, emissions from cattle, and so forth. Fortunately, we can address all of these problems without over-complicating the issue.

Making communities resilient is entirely sensible. As we will discover, though, the processes that help us stop burning fossil fuels can help us make progress on our resilience goals as well. The same can be said for the non-fossil fuel challenges. Cattle, for example, exhale and belch methane, which is a potent greenhouse gas. Their contribution to global warming is relatively small (roughly five percent), and research is underway that might make their contribution even smaller. Experiments have shown that adding a little bit of a certain seaweed to cow's diets reduces methane production by nearly 60 percent.[2] People are working on these problems from a number of different angles, and they deserve encouragement and support. They know that their work contributes to a more stable climate future. What we are looking for here, however, is a rubric that transforms our understanding of the climate crisis overall. Such a rubric can be found in tackling the most significant, widespread and relatable source of trouble. That source is unquestionably the combustion of fossil fuels.

Given how quickly we are approaching the 2°C threshold, we want to stop burning fossil fuels as soon as possible, certainly by 2040 to 2050. The IPCC projects that the next ten years will make all the difference because the cumulative buildup of carbon pollution in the atmosphere is the driving force behind global warming. The less carbon we add in total, the less warming will occur.[3]

You can also think in terms of managing a total carbon pollution budget. From this point of view, reducing emissions quickly minimizes the chances of an abrupt cut-off later when the budget suddenly runs out. If you have experience managing projects, you also know that starting early and front-loading your effort builds confidence and momentum, while providing more time to solve any problems that might crop up along the way. Starting early is wise because we do not want to fail in this quest; the consequences of failure are simply too horrific. The key to solving the climate crisis, therefore, boils down to a very simple statement:

Stop burning fossil fuels well before mid-century and absolutely, positively do not fail.

What changes when we accept this statement as our new premise? Nothing about Earth's physical and biological systems is altered by these words, but our perspective shifts on every aspect of the climate problem. A shift in perspective, it turns out, changes everything.

Why Is Having a Simple Premise so Important?

The wicked problem idea is a simple premise. Our new premise is equally simple. This matters a great deal because people always simplify. Thanks to evolution, simplifying is an inherent and necessary aspect of cognition. If your ancestors had been forced to think about their surroundings and the sounds in their ears every time a snake rattled or something breathed in the nearby bushes, you would not be here. Deliberative thought is a relatively slow process, too slow, in fact, for such dangers in the wild. The brain compensates by distilling past experiences into simple, familiar, quick emotional and physiological reactions. You hear a sound and before your conscious mind can identify what it is your bloodstream has been flooded with adrenaline and you have jumped away. You responded in an instant and you are ready for action.[4]

Just about everybody knows what this process feels like. An automated script protects you when, for example, you step into a crosswalk but suddenly jump back onto the curb before even realizing that a car is running the red light and might have hit you. People are sometimes embarrassed by this phenomenon too. You have probably seen someone who is normally calm and poised suddenly duck, shriek and slap their hands all over their neck because they felt something that the emotional brain recognized as "spider!" long before the conscious mind could do its analysis and exert control. Perhaps this has happened to you. It has happened to me more than once.

This process of rapid, simplified recognition and behavioral scripts evolved in the wild, but it is still active in our modern lives today. We use it all the time when we react to people's faces on the street, to the sound of the telephone, to the name on an email, to the timbre of someone's voice, to a puff of wind and, importantly, to some of the more complex problems that we face. Because we simplify based on accumulated experiences, we make an unconscious assumption that new experiences will be like past experiences. If a reaction worked in the past, the brain's fast-thinking processes conclude that it must have done something right, so the brain uses it again. Gonzales calls this "An ancient and universal strategy: automating activities for the sake of efficiency."[5]

People simplify because it works, not because it is perfect. This means that we do not always simplify appropriately. People are simplifying inappropriately, for example, when they say the climate crisis is only a problem for future generations to solve because the weather looks OK today. People simplify inaccurately when they believe that scientists disagree about the reality and causes of global warming. This view is wrong, but according to a survey in 2018, only 15 percent of the U.S. public sees the mistake.[6] If global warming was a benign non-issue, the inaccuracies probably would not matter very much. But climate change is an existential crisis, so the stakes are very high.

What percentage, for example, of climate scientists do you think agree that human caused global warming is occurring? Based on extensive evidence, about 97 percent have reached this conclusion.[7] How distant do you think the negative impacts of climate change are? Scientists have already identified global warming as a contributor to recent wildfires, intensified storms and the wave of climate refugees from Central America who traveled northward through Mexico to reach the U.S. southern border in 2019.[8]

Simplifying in counterproductive ways can lead to devastating results for people and communities. Simplifying accurately and in productive ways, on the other hand, can shift people's perspectives and behavior and help people discover new opportunities. To see this shift in action we need to apply our new, simple premise to the climate challenge itself. When we do this, the myriad ways in which we want to stop using fossil fuels look much more amenable to solutions. Instead of a wicked thicket of hopelessly entangled systems, the challenge boils down to a few simple and very practical questions.

From Helplessness to Hopeful Empowerment

The simple premise is *Stop burning fossil fuels well before mid-century and absolutely, positively do not fail.*

With this in mind, every decision that people make in the normal course of living their lives now has a companion question: how shall we do this without burning so much coal or oil or natural gas? The question is powerful in its simplicity. It expresses an imperative, but it does not undermine the value of the things we are doing in the first place. Reducing global warming becomes a companion priority in everyday life, business management and political affairs.

Such a simple question begets a few other, very pragmatic, questions too. For example, how shall we finance whatever investments we might want to make? How will we recognize the benefits that pay us back? What additional and surprising benefits will we gain by not burning so much fossil fuel? How can we let others know about the new benefits we enjoy? In organizational and civic decision-making, who gets to answer these questions, who is empowered to make the decisions and how do we want those decisions to be made?

These are empowering questions. By focusing on a single metric and everyday choices, we have broken a hopelessly entangled wicked problem into bite-sized decisions that everyone can relate to in their lives as consumers, family members, coworkers, leaders and citizens. You might not know how to manage global energy demand, but you do know that opening the windows on a pleasant day will reduce your energy costs. You also know that many people can buy electric power from a rooftop solar installer for less than it costs to buy it from the local utility company. Transforming global supply chains might seem terribly complex, but you can certainly figure out how to reduce your organization's shipping needs. Nobody knows how to decarbonize a nation's entire economy, but you can figure out some rules and incentives that will encourage citizens, communities and organizations to get creative and get the job done.

When viewed from this new perspective, reducing global warming appears to hinge on choices that are more local and easier for people, organizations, communities and governments to make. We have transformed the way *in which we think about the climate crisis* from a hopelessly complex, top-down engineering-style model to a much more localized and adaptive model. This new model, in turn, can transform the anxiety that so many people feel about the climate crisis into an attitude of empowerment and increased confidence.

Here's the issue: solving a wicked problem is difficult, in part, because nobody has control over all of the entangled and interacting systems. The puzzle, in other words, is not one that any single person, organization or government can solve. In reality, the solutions encompass all of the choices made by every nation, every organization and people who live in communities all over the world.

If the premise for reducing global warming seems to require a master plan and central control, then helplessness and frustration are the only possible outcomes. No such control exists, nor has it ever existed at any time in all of human history. A step forward in one location might be offset by a step backward somewhere else. I have heard countless arguments that the inability to control what other nations do implies there is no point making an effort here, or anywhere else for that matter. These arguments express a particularly discouraging form of cost-benefit analysis that says, "Why should we try if it might not work?"

The obvious answer is that inaction can only lead in one direction. The result will be a situation that the international community and a majority of people say they are eager to avoid. Taking action is the only viable alternative. A less obvious answer is that people will gain enormous benefits from the actions that they take regardless of what others decide to do. Recent studies by the Regional Greenhouse Gas Initiative (RGGI) in the Northeastern United States, for example, have shown that reducing carbon pollution significantly improved public health, avoided 39,000 lost days of work and saved $5.7 billion in healthcare costs.[9] The RGGI study teaches us something useful, which is that reducing carbon pollution where you live will make the people who live in your community healthier while lowering their cost of living.

The Paris Agreement on climate change embraces this obvious lack of central control. The agreement has been called groundbreaking not because the commitments are legally binding—they are not—nor because the goals are as ambitious as they could be. The accomplishment is that 195 nations agreed to something. In this case, they agreed to a common goal and a multi-lateral framework that embraces diffuse and varied approaches to decision-making.

When you think about climate change in this way, as an adaptive problem, you find yourself paying closer attention to different things. The entangled systems have not gone away, but decisions made locally by individuals, organizations, communities, informal networks, trade associations and other human communities take center stage. Local knowledge and hard-won experience are not merely curious anecdotes, they are prized resources. They are, in fact, the raw materials for larger-scale action. Overarching leadership might be beneficial, but as we have seen in the COVID-19 pandemic, local and regional governments are capable of learning from one another and acting accordingly when there is no alternative.

In an adaptive model, we recognize that there are many different solutions to be tried in many different circumstances. We want to encourage rapid, creative experimentation so we can fail quickly, succeed quickly, share knowledge, abandon things that do not work and amplify those that do. Public policies can and often do support this approach. Any type of financial incentive or disincentive, such as putting a price on carbon pollution, is intended to stimulate innovation and behavioral change. Under a cap and trade program or a carbon tax that increases over time, businesses and consumers pay increasingly high penalties for polluting. Such policies do not tell anybody how to reduce emissions or, for that matter, whether to reduce pollution at all. The policies merely impose a surcharge for polluting that increases year by year. Businesses and consumers, then, are free to invent ways to reduce emissions and save money. Their choices will create new knowledge, technologies and services that, in turn, will reveal new opportunities for reducing emissions even more as time goes by.

Regulatory approaches can accomplish the same goals. For example, during the 2020 Democratic Party primaries, presidential candidate Elizabeth Warren proposed requiring publicly traded corporations to disclose their climate-related vulnerabilities to investors. Such a policy would amount to another form of adaptive incentive. Corporations would not be required to reduce their vulnerabilities to rising sea levels, extreme heat and air pollution, flooding or any other climate-related risks, but investors would be able to see those risks and value the businesses differently. Presumably, the businesses would look for ways to enhance their value.[10]

Jonathan Koomey is a scientist who advises technology entrepreneurs on ways to reduce global warming. He agrees that the climate crisis is, by its very nature, an adaptive challenge. National, state and local policies can shift the playing field in beneficial ways, but the transition to a carbon-neutral world cannot be sorted out from the top down. Trying to align all the threads of an entangled wicked problem into a comprehensive picture looks like a fool's errand. Koomey argues that a faster and more effective approach involves experimentation, learning as we go and looking for the next opportunities as they emerge.[11]

Implicit in this idea—and critical to inspiring hope about our future—is the recognition that we do not need to figure out how to solve the entire problem at the outset. The truth is, nobody has ever decarbonized a global economy before. We are in unfamiliar territory here. Nobody is actually trying to master plan this transition either. Even the Paris Agreement calls upon each nation to determine how it will meet its own emissions targets. There really is no such thing as a comprehensive plan to solve the climate crisis. Whereas the wicked problem premise seems to imply that a comprehensive plan is needed if we are to believe in our future, the adaptive model accurately describes the future as a series of opportunities that have yet to be discovered and exploited.

Koomey describes how a simple change in property rights, for example, can create new and unforeseen opportunities. Suppose farmers are granted property rights to the airspace above their fields. In other words, suppose they can be paid for the electricity that can be generated by the wind that blows over their crops. Rules can be written to protect migrating birds and sensitive habit, but the basic idea is that a simple change in property rights can transform rural economies and accelerate the transition to clean energy. Presumably, more farmers would earn additional income while contributing more renewable energy to the grid. What new opportunities might follow from this increased wealth? Could farm subsidies be reduced or eliminated without harming some of the nation's growers? How might the economies and settlement patterns in rural states and communities change? Would the cost of wind energy drop even further than it already has, and would new manufacturing jobs be created?[12]

We can make assumptions and best guesses, but we cannot possibly predict everything that would ensue. As Koomey points out, experts tend to underestimate the hidden potential of adaptive approaches to change because economic models are not capable of accounting for innovation. This is actually good news. The future might be much brighter than we think it can be. These are just a few examples from the world of public policy, but other sectors of society are equally important in an adaptive approach. Koomey points out that the entrepreneur's job is to disrupt markets with innovations that make people want to abandon their old ways of doing things. Elon Musk and Tesla have become wildly famous, for example, for disrupting people's perceptions of electric vehicles. Tesla introduced the Model S luxury sedan in 2012, and Edmonds responded with

Not only is the 2012 Tesla Model S the best electric car you can buy today, it's also one of the best luxury sedans available. Forget everything you once knew of electric cars. The 2012 Tesla Model S has rewritten the rule book and may have even set the bar higher for conventionally powered cars.[13]

This is what entrepreneurs are going for. Tesla wants you to abandon your gasoline-powered investment happily and right away in favor of a new technology that you will genuinely want to buy. Successful carbon-friendly products and services need not involve sacrifices. In fact, they will fail if they do. Successful innovations will be more attractive than their climate-hostile competitors for a variety of reasons: they will be less expensive or more convenient, more enjoyable, more durable or some combination thereof. Each disruptive product or service, in turn, creates new opportunities. This, too, is good news.

Technology and public policy sometimes go hand-in-hand. Koomey describes how a policy in Germany that paid homeowners for the electricity generated on their rooftops encouraged sales and helped drive down the cost of solar for everyone else. As a result, rooftop solar became available to more and more people.[14] Policies that encourage innovation expand the range of opportunities, which is more good news.

Everything can and does change, from policies to technologies, costs, benefits, public attitudes and desires and social norms. No single factor or sector of society can get the entire job done on its own, and none has to. From an adaptive perspective, each has a great deal to offer as long as we keep the simple goal in mind:

Stop burning fossil fuels well before mid-century and absolutely, positively do not fail.

Our new premise is simple because there is only one thing to accomplish; it is actionable because it helps people make practical choices; and it is universal because it applies to people's personal lives, their job performance, to civic and political decision-making and to the ways we think and talk about global warming.

Rethinking and finding new ways to talk about the climate crisis is surprisingly important because it makes everyone a potential messenger of good news that can build public confidence. A communication researcher at George Mason University named Edward Maibach came to the climate issue from a background in public health. His simple mantra for changing our collective attitude goes like this: "Simple messages, repeated often, by a variety of trusted sources."[15] Our new premise about global warming encourages more and more people to stop feeling like victims and become trusted sources in their own right.

When we approach the climate crisis from this perspective, everybody's creativity is an asset, and inclusive approaches to decision-making make sense. The more people we engage in the process, the more knowledge we can acquire, the more we can accelerate progress and the more value we can create. Enthusiasm can grow and be more widespread as we build positive momentum and a greater sense of hope. People's sense of self-efficacy is likely to increase when they recognize that life is becoming better along the way.

Using a Simple "Stretch Goal" to Empower Change

Another term for this way of thinking comes from an in-depth study of corporations that have made surprisingly rapid improvements in their environmental performance. According to authors Daniel Esty and Andrew Winston, organizations make the most progress when they set "stretch goals" and declare that failure is not an option. A stretch goal is a clear, measurable goal that looks impossible at the outset. Stretch goals are effective because they disrupt people's assumptions about how things must be done: "Stretch goals drive creativity by asking the near impossible and demanding the reexamination of assumptions. They force everyone to search for new ways to meet old needs."[16]

Our new premise is, in fact, our new stretch goal. It has only one objective. It applies one and only one metric to every decision people need to make: *stop using fossil fuels*. There is a time-certain by which the goal needs to be achieved: *well before mid-century*. The last phrase says that "no" is not an option: *and absolutely, positively do not fail*.

We have seen how this new premise and an adaptive mentality can change our perspective on the value of many different public policy choices. Esty and Winston's study goes in a slightly different direction and demonstrates how effective these strategies have proven to be for individual organizations, which is where so many important carbon-cutting decisions are made. The authors found that when corporations employed stretch goals, they tended to exceed their goals by wide margins and beat the clock, often by several years.

Encouraged by their research, I decided to experiment with using a stretch goal strategy to see if I could de-carbonize the operations in a small business that I happened to own. I am referring to a design firm that I founded in the late 1980s.

In 2007, I signed up with The Climate Registry to have our

emissions verified by a third party, and we set 2006 as our baseline year.[17] As I thought about what goals to set, I looked to California's landmark Global Warming Solutions Act of 2006 (AB32), which was the most aggressive carbon mitigation law in the nation at the time. AB32 required the state to reduce economy-wide carbon pollution to 1990 levels by the year 2020. This meant a 30 percent reduction versus business-as-usual projections. The law also set a target for almost total decarbonization by the year 2050. Since my company did not own any long-lived capital equipment that we needed to amortize slowly, over decades, I decided to try to meet AB32's mid-century target much sooner. In other words, I wanted to shoot for a 90 percent emissions reduction by the year 2020. I also set ambitious targets for waste reduction and water use, as well, and announced to the staff that failure would not be an option. One member of the team literally asked if I had gone crazy. I took this as a good sign.

Like most people, I had no idea where to begin or how much money to invest. Being a small company with only twelve employees, we lacked the resources to hire expensive consultants who could help us. I made a number of false starts, beginning with bids to build a solar carport and a highly reflective metal roof. The architecture of our facility made both ideas far too expensive. I did trade the company car for a hybrid and our electric utility company offered free lightbulbs. Beyond these two actions, though, I seemed to be hitting nothing but brick walls.

I found the experience extremely frustrating, but I eventually came to realize that using stretch goals gave us an important adaptive advantage that was not apparent right away. An architect colleague helped me unlock the puzzle. He recommended that we start by trying to reduce our energy demand as much as possible before even considering things like rooftop solar. The idea was that if we reduced our energy needs, we would reduce the size and cost of solar power and any other systems that we might want to buy if we still found them necessary at all.

The architect's advice became our core strategy, and it led to a new company-wide policy. Since every organization makes practical, operational decisions every day, why not make energy efficiency a co-top priority in each and every one of them? I'm talking about the choices that business owners, managers and other employees are already making anyway. In other words, solving our carbon pollution problem stopped being a separate, overwhelmingly confusing and onerous task that had to be sorted out by people who were already preoccupied with running the company. Instead, every decision that we would ordinarily make now had two equal criteria: one was the business objective that had always been important and the other was to meet that objective in the most energy efficient way possible. We even came up with a slogan for our new approach: *"Make every decision a green decision."*

The similarity between this slogan and our new premise— *Stop burning fossil fuels well before mid-century and absolutely, positively do not fail*—is worth pointing out. The premise led to the company's stretch goal. The slogan—*Make every decision a green decision*—was our adaptive, tactical methodology and an easy-to-remember guideline for getting the job done.

Our new policy was also an example of what Chip and Dan Heath call widening the spotlight in order to consider additional information and widening the frame through which we looked at the problem in the first place. The results were absolutely astonishing. I honestly thought we might have reduced carbon pollution by ten or fifteen percent, which did not impress me. I was, in fact, discouraged and worried that we were failing. Imagine my surprise when, according to our verified emissions report, we slashed carbon pollution from on-site electricity and natural gas, and from the gasoline used in the company car, by a total of two-thirds. We achieved this result in less than eighteen months. Our electricity usage, for example, was cut in half, but nobody could tell that anything had changed. All we did was squeeze out waste that had previously been invisible to us. Nobody had to suffer or make a sacrifice. In fact, we managed to improve our quality of life.[18]

When I set about analyzing the costs and benefits, I widened the spotlight again. From the reading I had done, it appeared that most companies calculated the return on their eco-investments by looking at the money they saved on energy bills. This struck me as too narrow. Small differences in energy costs held little interest, so I decided to calculate all of the costs and savings associated with each of the carbon-cutting decisions we made. The hybrid car, for example, had lower service and insurance costs than the car it replaced, so those were added up. A new color copier allowed us to decommission other printers and plotters, so the savings on paper, ink, toner and maintenance went into the mix, and so on. In total, the company saved $9,000 annually, and these emissions and cost reductions held steady for many years.

It is fair to point out that our emissions were never more than a drop in the global bucket, but this misses the point. The lesson of Bowman Design Group's experiment is that an adaptive problem-solving approach that is based on a simple stretch goal proved to be surprisingly effective. It also validated a larger point, which is that people and organizations take a great deal of wasted energy for granted. All that waste can be eliminated quickly, painlessly and cost-effectively by every household, organization and community. In my experience, top-down approaches overlook the capacity of individuals and organizations to innovate. Top-down master plans also fail to energize and empower people to become the creators of their own climate destiny.

If the larger goals are to establish a new culture of informed empowerment and use it to tackle the climate crisis, then there is still more to learn from Bowman Design Group's story. Not long after receiving the good news about our emissions reductions, the company was recognized by the California Air Resources Board with a statewide small business of the year award. We issued a press release and two surprises followed.

The first was a call that came from our biggest corporate client. She said, "I saw the story and I had to call to say how proud we are to work with a supplier who would do something like this voluntarily." Surveys show that the public is increasingly worried about global warming, and we discovered that there is a deep wellspring of goodwill available to organizations that take climate action seriously. In my company's experience, people are willing to reward peers and organizations that lead the way.

The second surprise was a mess I found when I walked into the office one day. Every creative agency has a library of resource materials; binders stuffed full of samples and catalogs. They had come off the shelves and were spread all over the floor. When I asked what was going on the answer came back, "We decided to rearrange everything so the most sustainable materials would be at eye level." This was a sign that employees were experiencing a new sense of purpose, ownership and commitment to the business. Other examples of pride and initiative soon followed, proving, again and again, that people are looking for more out of life than just a paycheck. There is a genuine hunger to be part of something meaningful. When leaders commit themselves to solving the climate crisis, good things happen; morale improves and productivity increases, as a sense of personal ownership takes hold. Employees, it turns out, have become a potent source of pressure on corporations of every size to improve environmental performance.[19]

Using an adaptive strategy that is based on a stretch goal yields many surprises. For example, my company's employees commuted to work, just as everyone else does. Two of our employees, in particular, relocated to Palm Springs, more than one hundred miles from our office. Together, they made the horrendous drive from Palm Springs to the Long Beach area every day, usually during the commuter rush hour that choked Southern California's freeways. Making matters worse, one or two employees would often leave the office during the middle of the day and drive a substantial distance to meet with a supplier, and then drive back to the office before commuting all the way home. These trips consumed a great deal of time and left people feeling exhausted, which translated into longer hours and greater stress about meeting deadlines. We lived with these apparent "realities" for years because we never thought seriously about them. As crazy as this seems in hindsight, the fatigue, stress, pollution and lost productivity seemed to be inherent, or at least tolerated, aspects of doing business.

The "stop burning fossil fuels" imperative made us look at every process differently. It changed our fast-thinking assumption that we must have been doing something right all along. We decided, instead, to try an experiment. Our long-distance commuters would only travel one day per week and supplier visits would be scheduled early and late in the day to coincide with commuting. In most cases, the supplier visits would be made by whoever's commuting route came closest to the supplier's facility. The reductions in carbon pollution that followed are part of what is called "scope three" emissions, and unfortunately, our third-party verification system did not measure them. In other words, we reduced total carbon pollution by more than two-thirds, but I do not know the full extent of our success. I do know that employee mileage compensation fell by more than half. More importantly, however, I heard much more laughter in the office and people seemed genuinely more relaxed.

In other words, working from the premise that global warming is a simple problem (and it is our problem to solve), and using an adaptive approach (everything gets re-examined and every idea is worth considering) toward a clear and ambitious stretch goal (quickly stop using fossil fuels) solved a surprising number of other problems that we had assumed were intractable. We became a healthier, happier and better-connected group of people and a more productive company. There is nothing particularly unique about Bowman Design Group's circumstances. The benefits we enjoyed are available to anyone else who wants them.

Bowman Design Group did something incredibly simple: we hung our mental picture of the climate crisis upside down. When we did so, everything looked different. Even in the relatively limited context of our business operations we set aside a debilitating wicked problem premise and discovered unexpected and valuable benefits. This is how we, collectively, can turn a seemingly hopeless entanglement of complex systems into practical and manageable everyday challenges. The guiding question for every decision by individuals, organizations and governments is how to do the things we need to do but do them without using fossil fuels.

Adaptive approaches put solutions closer to where people live and where the positive or negative implications are actually felt. Low-carbon solutions for agriculture, buildings, urban planning and transportation, energy generation, waste management and other systems involve practical choices that can yield unimagined benefits. And since the people whose lives are most impacted by the decisions are also the creative agents of their own futures, an adaptive strategy has the potential to help overcome structural inequities that continue to expose low income communities and people of color to the most harm.

If we look at the COVID-19 crisis from this perspective, we discover that amidst the anxiety and tragedy there are opportunities to reduce global warming. Global emissions decreased when economies shut down and more people stayed home.[20] The reduction in driving led to cleaner air and quieter streets. People who had the luxury of working from home started talking about feeling less stressed and more comfortable. A majority (59%) of those who were able to work from home due to the pandemic said in the summer of 2020 that they had no desire to return to their old patterns of commuting and working in office buildings.[21] Expectations shifted quickly as more and more people experienced, and then came to defend, a new status quo.

These changes happened rapidly. The "safer at home" experiment is still new, but the longer it continues the more peoples' expectations are likely to change. A great many businesses might not need so much extensive and expensive real estate in the future. New business opportunities are likely to emerge, but it is impossible to predict in advance what they will look like.

Did you see stories about people in Italy singing together from their balconies during the harshest days of the epidemic? Did you hear New Yorkers clapping their appreciation for healthcare workers each night when hospital shifts changed? People seek fulfillment and social connection under any circumstances; connection and fulfilment are not the exclusive property of the fossil fuel-driven status quo.

While the premise that says global warming is a "wicked problem" encourages people to dismiss incremental progress as trivial and merely anecdotal, the alternative premise that says the climate crisis is a "simple problem" tends to focus attention on new opportunities wherever they happen to be. When viewed from this perspective, we can see many encouraging signs. The costs of new renewable energy, for example, keep dropping year over year, which drives double-digit growth in the clean energy sector.[22] The World Bank stopped funding new fossil fuel development projects after 2019,[23] and the European Development Bank agreed to follow suit in 2021.[24] After a devastating tornado damaged or destroyed 95 percent of the buildings in the small farm town of Greensburg, Kansas in 2007, the community elected to rebuild as a model green city.[25] Iowa got more than 40 percent of its electricity from clean wind energy in 2019.[26] The list of positive developments continues to grow.

More importantly, the COVID-19 pandemic has demonstrated just how quickly old expectations can be abandoned. This is a hopeful sign, too, but human behavior is always complex. Coal production and use, for example, remain high throughout the world. We have seen that, with clear guidance, people can change their behavior overnight. Humanity, for example, responded to "flatten the curve" en masse. Conversely, we have seen how destructive it can be when people simplify inappropriately. Flattening the curve is not the same thing as eliminating the coronavirus, but in the summer of 2020 many people behaved as if the virus had already been defeated.

There is no reason to think that social change should advance in a straight line. Setbacks are part of the process, yet we can still be inspired to pursue the things we care about. The silver lining of this dark pandemic has been improved air quality over major cities. As the RGGI studies showed, cutting emissions yields significant improvements in people's health right away, and people are now experiencing this reality firsthand. In addition, those who are able to work from home are enjoying reductions in commuter and workplace stress. Everybody, meanwhile, is witnessing spontaneous adaptations to physical distancing that actually increase social connectedness.

There are reasons to be hopeful that people can create the societies they want to live in. How can we help people come to believe in this new premise? Unlike the corporations that set stretch goals for themselves, diverse and democratic societies are not required to follow a chief executive's lead. Nobody is assigning a stretch goal to the nation. Are there other ways to help people activate this strategy? The next chapters will explore ways to create a culture of empowerment from within.

Chapter 3

A View from the Front Lines

As is probably clear by now, I am neither a climate scientist nor an educator, nor a policy expert, finance expert, politician, international negotiator, journalist or academic researcher in social psychology and communication theory. I am an entrepreneur and business owner, and a communication practitioner who focuses primarily on strategic planning and creative media. Most of my work involves organizing and managing complex projects in marketing or informal education at museums and public aquariums.

People who do this type of work bring a particular lens to social change. We tend to work outside of—and often in between—professions and institutions. Communicating is an important thing for any institution to do well, so communication practitioners gain deep exposure to an unusually wide variety of organizations and their cultures, world views, concerns and hypotheses about how to encourage people to engage with new ideas and information.

Communication practitioners play the cards that are dealt by their clients, target audiences and society. Generally speaking, our task is to change people's knowledge and understanding or perceptions and behaviors in the near term and sometimes right in the moment. From our perspective, communication is always competitive, meaning that our clients vie for people's attention.

This competition takes place in circumstances that are constantly changing. People's priorities and opinions and the material circumstances in which they live are dynamic. In the summer of 2019, for example, the unemployment rate in the United States was 3.6 percent. Eleven months later, in April of 2020, that number had leapt to 14.7 percent and a global pandemic was underway.[1] People were sheltering in place and losing their jobs or going to work despite fears that doing so would make their loved ones and themselves gravely ill. Shifts such as these make enormous differences in people's priorities. Yesterday's hot button issue gets pushed off the front burner by something more urgent.

Within this ever-changing context, my work involves combing through the complexity of a challenge to find the crux. The crux is that key insight, that new kernel of knowledge, that unexpected way of organizing and clarifying information or that surprising experience that unlocks a puzzle and helps people see things in new ways. Communication practitioners like me hone their combing skills though countless assignments over many years. But sometimes the crux drops right into your lap.

Technically speaking, I am talking about an epiphany. Outside of a religious context, an epiphany is a moment of revelation or a sudden insight into some aspect of reality. True epiphanies tend to change people's lives and reorder their priorities. They can pack quite an emotional charge as well, which makes the experience easy to relive many years later, but very difficult to forget.

This story begins, for me, in the early 2000s, when I received my education in climate science. It came by way of a communication project and the generosity of eminent researchers and interpreters at the National Academy of Sciences. In order to explain global warming to the public, I found it necessary to understand the material at some depth. I recall being concerned at the time about what the scientific evidence implied. The prevailing attitude among the scientists, however, seemed to be that humanity still had time to make wise decisions and avoid significant harm.

Just a few years later, my company and I were working with another group of the world's leading climate scientists on another exhibition. I sensed immediately that the mood was different. In 2006, the rate of melting in the Arctic accelerated significantly. Global carbon emissions were also rising at a rate that would later prove to match or exceed the worst-case scenario that the Intergovernmental Panel on Climate Change had studied. Until that point in time, the worst-case had been considered outside the bounds of anything humanity would allow to happen. Rapid industrialization in Asia, combined with relatively little progress on emissions reductions elsewhere, was quickly driving emissions higher than anybody had foreseen.

All of this was context for an exhibition planning meeting in early 2007. I was sitting in a conference room located high on a bluff overlooking the Pacific Ocean in Southern California. The sun was shining, and the view was spectacular. The project scientist and I were discussing content for the exhibition and, almost in passing, I said, "The folks at the National Academies told me to keep an eye on the ocean. They said the ocean can absorb so much heat before temperatures rise that when the water temperature finally does begin to increase, we'll be committed to a global warming for maybe five hundred to one thousand years."

"Oh," she said, "we're part of Project Argo, and we've already measured warming in every ocean basin in the world to a depth of one thousand meters."

Stop, for a moment, and think about what this means. Nearly four-fifths of the planet is covered by the ocean, and all of that water has already warmed to a depth of more than three thousand feet. The amount of heat required to warm that much water is hard to imagine.

I always find the next moment of that day difficult to describe. Words just can't do it justice. In a flash, everything that I understood about the impacts of global warming—the social disruptions, economic upheaval, crop failures, famine, mass migrations, violent conflicts, failed states, wildfires, floods, drought, coastal inundation and mass extinction—all of it came home to roost, all at once. These horrors and tragedies had seemed concerning but still quite distant until that moment. Suddenly, out of the blue, they were alive, and they were inside that conference room with us. Global warming was no longer some far-off concern. It was already well underway, and it was here to stay.

The hairs literally stood up on the back of my neck. It felt like something primeval; a visceral warning more serious and imminent than anything I have ever felt. It was more complex than just fear; it was dread, grief and surprise, too, and a need to do something quickly. I could feel its presence and I wanted to turn around and look, but nothing would be there. I was finding it difficult to breathe, and I had no idea how to carry on with the conversation. Did the scientists know this? Did anybody? Why did they seem so calm? I felt utterly disrupted. Everything had stopped, and I struggled to get a purchase on my familiar roles as a science interpreter and supplier and business owner, all of which had been stripped away in a naked moment.

In the silence, she carried on with something else: "By the way, my boss is here, and she'd like to meet you now."

Anyone who has ever owned a business knows that when you meet your client for the first time you want to be cool. Your mission is to feel confident and reassuring. No challenge is too great. Nothing is ever a problem. But when I walked into her office and sat down, I was still trying to gather myself. I think I was actually trembling. We chatted briefly about the project and then she looked at me quietly and asked, "Is there anything you want to ask me?"

"Yes," I said. "How do you cope with knowing what you know?"

"Ah," she said, as if we could now get down to the real business. She spoke for a few minutes about humanity's prospects. I recall her saying, "The question is how many other species we're going to take with us." I must have wondered aloud about the futility of building a small exhibition in the face of something so massive; a threat that nobody other than the scientists seemed to know anything about. She replied that connecting people with global warming science was good work to be doing, but I couldn't resolve the cognitive dissonance between the scale of the world and the scope of our little project.

This was the beginning of a new journey for me. On the long drive home, I wondered if there was any way to unlearn what I had just learned and go back to my life as it had been an hour earlier. The answer to a question like this is always "no." I quickly realized a few other important things as well.

The first was that there is no job title "Reducer of Global Warming." My impression was that if everyone did their jobs extremely well, we still might not tackle the climate crisis. Accomplishing something as unusual as decarbonizing the global economy seemed to require going above and beyond the limits of our job descriptions, thinking outside the proverbial box and being willing to take some risks. While I still think this is essentially true, I would amend the statement today by saying that if people do their jobs with "stop using fossil fuels" as their central objective, then we will be on the right track.

The second insight was that the back-and-forth nature of national politics will always undermine our capacity to make rapid and lasting progress toward stabilizing the climate system. When, two years later, I met a lobbyist who was trying to get a climate bill through the U.S. Congress, he said with surprise, "You want to change culture!" I think this is a sensible objective. If we can create a culture of informed commitment and empowerment, we will reduce the extremes of political ping-ponging and move more quickly and steadily toward the future that people say they want. I am not saying that everyone needs to agree about which policies are best. Changing our culture is about something more fundamental. It is about establishing a deeper and more widespread expectation that our job is to stop using fossil fuels quickly and that we can do this job well.

Third, I was keenly aware that if solving the climate crisis depended on encouraging everyone to experience the depth of emotional shock and discomfort that I experienced, we would get nowhere. The question, therefore, is whether we can help people understand what needs to be done and motivate action without driving people toward gloom and despair? The answer, as we will see below and in the next chapter, is an emphatic yes.

Fourth, when I looked around in 2007, I struggled to find other communication professionals who knew very much about global warming and the underlying science. I also realized that I needed to learn a great deal more about behavioral psychology and decision science as well as about what the social sciences had to say on the topic of communicating about risks. In other words, I needed to become a sponge and learn everything I could while also building stronger relationships with climate scientists, economists, communication strategists and a variety of other content experts.

Last, I realized that owning a business provided an unusual and valuable opportunity. My business could become a laboratory for experimenting with ways to reduce the organization's carbon footprint. I wanted to know if we could establish a credible and repeatable business case, in addition to the more obvious moral case, for slashing emissions. The success of this adventure was explained earlier, but there is one more crucial piece to that story.

Two years after earning recognition from the California Air Resources Board, I was asked to speak at the reception for a new group of small business honorees. I decided to drop the usual businessman façade and describe my motivations for decarbonizing the company in very personal terms. I talked about the epiphany, my halting attempts to decarbonize and my frustrations with our false starts. I described how our eventual success energized our team and changed our company's culture. I explained that I was not driven by a desire to improve business performance. I was motivated, instead, by my understanding of how dangerous the climate crisis is and by a sense of calling to do something about it.

To my great surprise, when I finished speaking, one of the honorees asked if she could say a few words, so I handed the microphone to her. She talked about her own motivations which, like mine, had nothing to do with business performance. She finished and another honoree asked to speak. His motivations were equally personal and heartfelt. The microphone continued its journey around the room, with each business owner bearing witness to something deeply personal. The microphone eventually came to a gentleman who began by saying, "I can't tell you how good it feels to finally be in a business meeting where I can talk about things that I really care about."

It was a relief to discover that my experiences, concerns and commitments were not unique or even particularly unusual. Just about everybody has heard of Greta Thunberg and the extraordinary work she is doing. She is not alone by any means. None of us is alone. Climate leaders can be found everywhere, in every profession and in just about every community. They fill every job description, they speak every language, they come in all ages, they are women and men and people from every race and ethnic background. And they have a lot of motivation and good ideas.

The abiding question for me, then, is how to marshal our true leaders and create a culture of informed empowerment. Are there any pressure points in our culture that are firm enough to press against and give a shove? The answer turns out to be "Yes, there are many."

But efforts to engage the public with the climate crisis have, so far, been dominated by two basic approaches. Scientists and science educators have been distributing the facts, while activists and social movements have been trying to make us care. This might be an oversimplification, but not enough attention has been paid to us, the audience. As decision scientist Baruch Fischhoff notes,

> It is impossible to judge people fairly or to provide them with needed information without knowing what is on their minds when they formulate, resolve, implement, and revise climate-related choices. Acquiring that knowledge requires research that is informed by climate science, decision science, and social science.[2]

When was the last time you made a decision solely on the basis of facts? That is not something that people do very often. When was the last time someone was able to make you truly care? That does not happen very often either.

The decisions people make are influenced by their assumptions and emotions and by the signals they get from the people around them. Each one of us is influenced by the leaders and messengers whom we trust and by what society seems to agree is important. And, as the unfortunate people who stood on the beach in Panang learned that fateful day, we tend to rely on our mental models and behavioral scripts even when new information says our ideas are wrong.

Andrew J. Hoffman, who studies culture, business and sustainability at the University of Michigan, puts it this way:

> Cultural identity can overpower scientific reasoning. When belief or disbelief in climate change becomes connected to our cultural identity, contrary scientific evidence can actually make us more resolute in resisting conclusions that are at variance with our cultural beliefs. ... In short, increased knowledge tends to strengthen our position on climate change, regardless of what that position is.[3]

Dispensing more information will not get the job done. Nor, it turns out, is it necessary to make everybody care.

We do not, in fact, even need to educate everybody. As noted earlier, people tend to defend the status quo, yet we adapt quickly if the situation changes. This means that carbon pollution can also be reduced by resetting default choices in favor of climate-friendly behavior.[4] Most people will just adapt and then defend the new status quo without giving it very much thought.

Given how complex our motivations can be, Fischhoff advises communication professionals to be humble and to take advantage of decision and behavioral science research:

> People overestimate how widely their values are shared. ... People overestimate how widely their knowledge is shared. ... People overestimate how clearly they communicate. ... Research protects scientists and citizens against such imperfect intuitions. ... Communicating entails listening as well as speaking. Research provides a way to do that listening.[5]

The type of research Fischhoff talks about is highly situational; it needs to be done for each new communication initiative that involves significant potential and financial cost. We encounter the climate crisis, after all, in the most over-communicated society the world has ever known. Although estimates vary widely, the average person in the United States is exposed to somewhere between five thousand and ten thousand messages each and every day.[6] The rate at which new data and information is being generated is equally staggering. In 2013, *Science Daily* reported that 90 percent of the world's data had been generated in just the previous two years.[7] This means that the competition for people's attention can be fierce. Efforts by the fossil fuel industry to intentionally mislead people, confuse the climate issue and dissuade people from paying attention must be added to this competitive mix as well.

As we grapple with how to build informed empowerment on the climate issue, we can learn a great deal from the researchers who explore these issues in depth and from fellow practitioners who, in effect, conduct practical experiments in how to break through the messaging clutter and help people connect.

Chapter 4

What Helps People Engage?

People have been working on social change for decades, and if you look at their efforts in total, they have made substantial progress. They have also fallen short. Educators and communication professionals are just like everyone else: in spite of our expertise, we are still human, and we suffer from the same limitations and biases that hold everybody back.

The confirmation bias, for example, which is the tendency to accept information that supports what we already believe, is one of our biggest problems. Too many grants fund too many outreach projects based on hunches and the conventional wisdom rather than hard evidence about the people we are trying to reach. Baruch Fischhoff noted that our ability to connect with people depends on listening and learning more about them. Just like everyone else, though, we can get busy, we run short of funds and we make assumptions. We are not immune from thinking that we know more about other people than we actually do. All too often, we fail to make learning what is on people's minds the top priority. In a few cases, I have even seen institutions turn their backs on audience questions and survey data in order to charge ahead with projects that reflected their own priorities and beliefs.

We can do better. The climate challenge will be won or lost inside people's minds, where their assumptions, beliefs, emotions and scripts will determine the future. This is no time for arrogance or complacency. It is a time for humility, listening and putting what we learn to better use.

The competition for attention is a good place to start because the competition is so fierce. We are up against a deluge of distracting issues—including unemployment, racism and a pandemic—that push climate change off the front burner. In addition, though, we are also competing against beliefs that discourage people and dissuade them from getting involved. Those beliefs are being actively manipulated and amplified, over and over again, through a disinformation campaign designed to confuse, mislead and emphasize feelings of helplessness and detachment. How can we compete against such a well-funded and strategically managed campaign? An adage from the world of brand management and marketing is designed for situations just like this.

If the Game is Rigged Against You, Change the Game.

Every strategic advantage also has an Achilles' heel, a weakness that is impossible to defend. We know what makes the disinformation campaign so strong; it is the drumbeat repetition of simple messages stoking resentment toward government and ideological opponents. These messages play to people's anxieties about the economy and their jobs and to the feelings of victimization that seem so widespread. Sowing doubt is easy to do when the weather seems fairly normal. People are confused, as well, about the degree of scientific agreement that today's weather is just a red herring. Just take a look around and ask yourself if everyone is acting concerned and talking about their desire to end the climate crisis. The answer is probably "no," and this gives the deniers their strength.

From a marketing communication perspective, debating and debunking such messages is a fool's errand. There is a more effective strategy, which is to ignore the false debate entirely. Make the reality of the climate crisis axiomatic and move on. Focus, instead, on increasing people's confidence that we can meet the climate challenge and achieve the quality of life that everybody wants.

The resources for making this type of strategic shift are abundant. Fifty-seven percent of the U.S. public says they are "alarmed" or "concerned" about global warming.[1] That number has been increasing and, as of 2020, is at an all-time high. Forty-one percent say they have experienced the changing climate first-hand.[2] Support for policies to promote clean energy and regulate carbon dioxide as a pollutant is strong across party lines.[3] In other words, a large majority of the American people already believes that global warming is a serious threat and wants something done about it. This is the Achilles' heel of the denial campaign. Don't help the deniers undermine these beliefs. Increase people's sense of hope and confidence, instead, by moving on to real solutions.

Organizations of every kind are already doing just that. The largest general science membership organization in the world, the American Association for the Advancement of Science, has issued a clear, concise statement about the reality of climate change.[4] Most of the world's medical and health organizations have issued a joint statement that calls climate change the greatest public health challenge facing humanity.[5] Thousands of leaders in city and state governments, businesses, faith-based and cultural organizations, universities and healthcare organizations have made commitments to meet the goals of the Paris Agreement within their spheres of influence. Together, these commitments represent 67 percent of U.S. gross domestic product, 65 percent of the population and 51 percent of U.S. carbon emissions.[6]

These resources point to the Achilles' heel of the doubt, inaction and despair agenda. The time has come to disengage from the game the deniers are playing. If needed, a simple statement settles the debate: "Based on extensive evidence, about 97 percent of climate scientists have concluded that human-caused global warming is occurring."[7] A better strategy, however, is simply to assume that everybody agrees climate change is real and move on to other matters. Doing so resets the status quo and gives the majority of people the opportunity to adapt quickly.

Leaving denial behind allows us to address society's single biggest challenge, which is a lack of confidence:

> There is strong evidence that four key beliefs—that global warming is happening, human caused, dangerous, and solvable—are important. Multiple studies show that among these four beliefs, low confidence in society's capacity to solve the climate challenge is the most significant missing ingredient.[8]

Moreover,

> There is strong evidence that, when it comes to global warming, people's sense of collective efficacy is very low. Americans are simply not convinced that society can solve the climate challenge. ... Researchers and practitioners alike strongly advised shifting away from doom-and-gloom forecasts to messages that build a sense of efficacy in the capacity of communities, the nation, and the world to solve the climate crisis.[9]

Shifting our basic premise away from the wicked problem narrative, which is inherently gloomy, to the premise that the climate crisis is a simple problem transforms the entire mental framework in a productive way.

It is equally important to recognize that nobody has all of the answers. Productive innovations always create new opportunities to take the next big steps. Speaking with confidence about humanity's capacity to meet adaptive challenges, which is what the climate crisis is, emphasizes society's intrinsic strength. The task, remember, is simple: *Stop burning fossil fuels well before mid-century and absolutely, positively do not fail.*

The time has come to build clear and compelling narratives

about humanity's ability to reduce global warming and avert the crisis. The components of such a narrative are abundant. The news media, for example, frequently reports stories about new technologies, falling costs for clean energy, new jobs in the clean economy, corporate commitments and so on. The themes underlying such stories can be knit together into a narrative about adaptive problem-solving that makes meaningful contributions to our common desire for cleaner air, cleaner water and healthier, more fulfilling lives.

Even today, in the dark shadows of a deadly global pandemic and skyrocketing unemployment, humanity demonstrates its capacity to respond quickly and appropriately to a crisis. At the same time, we are discovering the things that people really want, such as cleaner air, less traffic, stronger social connections and lower stress. These are the ingredients for creating a brighter future. That's the story.

Gloom-and-doom messages about global warming are counterproductive. Effective messages tend to make people feel better, not worse. Communication strategist Robert Gould puts it this way:

> Research demonstrates that, rather than the traditional carrot/ stick methodology, the most effective way to motivate change is through positive reinforcement. It's called the Shamu principle and has also been proven effective on husbands. In a word, make change fun.[10]

In Southern California, where I live, water is becoming a scarce commodity, so city leaders want people to replace thirsty lawns with more drought-tolerant and California-friendly landscapes. Getting the first household in a neighborhood to make the change is hard because someone has to break the status quo. Once that happens, though, other households follow suit, sparking a friendly competition that lets everyone enjoy beautiful and interesting front yards. People enjoy seeking what they want.

Recognize Who the Heroes Are

In 2008, political psychologist Jon Krosnick noted that the so-called "issue public" for climate change was one of the largest ever measured.[11] An issue public is that percentage of the population who could not possibly care more about an issue than they already do. When they are motivated, their commitment and energy change public policy. Spurred on by today's youth and climate justice movements, this segment of the population has the potential to become a powerful political force.

Author Joseph Campbell described the leaders among us in a different way. He wrote about an enduring narrative tradition that is based on the archetypical hero's journey. The hero, in classical mythology, is an ordinary person who is forced into a daunting challenge upon which everything depends. The path is difficult, and the trials seem insurmountable. The hero is destined to fail and hits rock bottom. In the moment of greatest need, a wise advisor gives the hero the crucial tool in the form of empowering advice, training in a skill or a magical object. Rising up from depths of despair, the hero emerges with greater determination than ever and defeats the great enemy. The hero then returns to the people with a gift of enormous value. If this story arc sounds familiar, that is because you have seen it countless times in popular novels and films.

Jonah Sachs, the creator of more than one viral video, notes that in the age of social media, the hero's journey is becoming an important framework for public outreach.[12] The broadcast era, in which only a handful of authoritative institutions had access to mass media outlets, has been replaced by a world in which people share messages with one another however they please. Influence is now more diffused and horizontal than it used to be. The nature of communication practice is changing according to the types of messages people want to receive and pass along.

Authenticity is a top priority because people are reluctant to share messages that seem manipulative or contrived.

Moreover, the institutions that once defined society's most important challenges are no longer the heroes. The institutions conducting public outreach—including government, scientists, news outlets and educators—are not the heroes either. They have become the wise advisors who can provide that special piece of knowledge and power in the hero's hour of need.

Who, then, are the heroes today? The marketing community is way ahead of the climate outreach community in figuring this out. A recent billboard by Nike, the apparel and athletic equipment giant, provided the answer in just four simple words. There were no pictures of the company's products or action photos of elite athletes in that ad. There were no superlative descriptions of incredible technologies or promises that winning breakthroughs lay ahead. The billboard simply said the following: *"Yesterday you said tomorrow."*

The customer is the hero in this ad. The fitness journey is hard, and the obstacles are many. Nobody wants to leave their warm bed before dawn to go for an exhausting run in the cold rain. The Nike brand is telling heroes everywhere that they understand. They acknowledge your human weakness and they honor your inherent strength. In fact, they remind you of your role as the hero of your own life's journey with a challenge: "Yesterday you said tomorrow."

The goal is to celebrate and empower people. As Robert Gould points out, successful communication campaigns also acknowledge that people will fail and then get back up again.[13] We build hope when we celebrate people's self-efficacy and when we remind ourselves that we can get back up again every time we fall.

Advertisers such as Nike are tapping into the hero's journey archetype in order to boost sales, but their insight into the relationship between experts and the rest of us applies equally to issues of urgent social concern. Today's messaging strategy needs to be a bold departure from the top-down approach, with its implication that only the experts can disentangle a wicked problem. Acknowledging that the people we communicate with are today's heroes is working so well that some of the world's most successful brands are staking their reputations and their futures on it. New Yorkers intuitively embraced the hero's journey archetype when they cheered and applauded exhausted healthcare workers night after night. Closer to home, I thanked a checkout clerk at the supermarket for working during the pandemic. She replied that she and her co-workers had never felt so appreciated. Have you felt compelled to do the same thing? Each of us knows what being down and out feels like and what getting back up again can do for the community and for the human spirit.

The gloomy wicked problem strategy, on the other hand, leaves people feeling powerless and ineffective. Worse still, if government, corporations and science institutions pretend to be the heroes, they expose themselves to resentment for having done so little to help.

When I think about celebrating climate leaders, I am reminded again and again of the people who own small businesses. These are people who accept uncertainty and self-determination as a way of life. They get knocked down by circumstances, and those who survive in business manage to get back up again, becoming stronger each time they do. Politicians like to tie themselves to the ethos of the entrepreneur when it is time to win votes, but, for the most part, the owners of small businesses know they are on their own. They do not speak with a unified voice because they are a fiercely independent and self-reliant group of people. They are important to a culture of empowerment, however, because according to the U.S. Census Bureau, small and medium-sized business enterprises, most of which are privately owned, generate roughly half of private sector employment in the

United States, about half of the nation's gross domestic product and nearly all of the new jobs.[14]

If these numbers surprise you, it is probably because the news media tends to ignore them. The media covers the stock market and the concentrations of wealth and power in the nation's largest corporations. The wealth and jobs created by small business entrepreneurs are equal to those of the corporate economy, but the jobs and wealth are diffused throughout cities, towns and rural areas everywhere. Characterizing the collective accomplishments of small and medium-sized enterprises or wrangling them in support of a common mission is difficult to do because they are located everywhere, they are not joiners by nature and they are too busy working to speak up. We miss an important opportunity to increase our sense of self-efficacy, however, when we buy into the myth that the corporate economy is the entire show. Half of us do not even work there.

In all my years as an entrepreneur and business owner, I have never had to answer to anonymous shareholders. I have answered to myself, my family and the employees with whom I worked closely every day. These relationships are personal and therefore extremely powerful. A small company is like a mirror that reflects your character and allegiances back to you almost on a daily basis. Like everyone else who owns a business, I made decisions and built a culture that reflected my values as much as they reflected the realities of the marketplace. As Gary Erickson, the founder of Clif Bar & Company wrote, "Business has a purpose beyond money. We look for meaning in our lives. Business has meaning too."[15]

We go into business because we have an idea and there is something we want to try to do. We stay in business because it gives us the opportunity to express ourselves and create lifestyles for ourselves and our employees that have intrinsic meaning. It is no surprise, then, that small businesses are also the economy's primary source of innovation. As Gary Erickson notes, "Successful entrepreneurs take who they are and what they already know and create surprising combinations."[16]

In my experience, which includes talking with a great many other business owners, the most important skills that we develop involve combining personal values and commitments with creative and intuitive problem solving. Society celebrates the success of innovative entrepreneurs such as Steve Jobs, Elon Musk, Ben Cohen, Jerry Greenfield, Yvon Chouinard and Gary Erickson. We should celebrate the millions of others, as well, who populate our communities. Their capacity to embrace the simplicity of the climate challenge—finding ways to stop using fossil fuels in the myriad decisions they make—and to move nimbly and quickly is difficult to overestimate. A survey of their accomplishments would be an inspiring thing to read.

If you want to harness this latent potential for action on global warming, the best strategy is probably to create an expectation among everyone else that the climate crisis is ours to solve. Entrepreneurs spend so much time listening to their customers and suppliers that they will hear the message. When they hear you, they will respond because that is what business owners do. A non-profit agency that promotes energy efficiency once told me that their greatest success came when middle school students went door to door in business neighborhoods asking the owners to use less energy. Who could look the kids in the eye and refuse? The rest of us, therefore, have the power to activate a sleeping giant.

Celebrate Our Diversity

The values that business owners care deeply about are as diverse as everyone else's, of course. Connecting with people on the climate challenge means connecting with the values they already hold. As Fischhoff pointed out earlier, "People overestimate how widely their values are shared."[17] It makes no sense, therefore, to assume that other people will adopt the values you hold dear.

Robert Gould, the principal strategist of the highly successful "Truth" antitobacco campaign, applies this insight about campaigns that try to change social norms.

> The majority of social campaigns (and political ones) try to convince their target audience to do what "we" think they should do. The campaigns that work are the ones that don't try to convince or educate the audience, but genuinely connect with them.[18]

You might have seen presentations and documentaries or read books about the climate crisis, plastic pollution, wildlife extinction or other issues that conclude that "we must all" agree to something. However well intended, admonitions like these ask everyone to think alike, revere nature in the same way or support the philosophical underpinnings of certain policy frameworks. These are non-starters for most people. Values are deeply held and difficult to change. The goal, remember, is to make people feel better, not worse.

The notion that everyone should adopt the same worldview runs counter to the evidence. In the United States, for example, global warming has fallen into the partisan divide, but prominent conservatives are just as committed to tackling the problem as progressives. Former Republican Congressman Bob Ingles, for example, founded the Energy and Enterprise Institute to promote conservative solutions to global warming. Rebranded as republicEN, Ingles' organization promotes the idea of a tax on carbon pollution in which the revenue is returned to consumers. The idea is to give consumers the choice of paying more for carbon-intensive products or saving money by choosing lower-cost, clean energy alternatives. The republicEN team makes a compelling case that responding to the climate crisis is necessary and that it can be done while supporting the small government, free market values that conservatives share.[19]

The solution to the climate crisis is not embedded in a particular set of values. The solution is simple and straightforward: *Stop burning fossil fuels well before mid-century and absolutely, positively do not fail.*

As noted earlier, in society's response to an adaptive challenge nobody has all the answers. The creativity that is expressed through our diversity holds the keys to efficient, effective, just and enjoyable solutions. Celebrating the different values that drive this process forward is, in fact, an essential part of the program.

Align Reason and Emotions and Clear the Path

A culture of climate empowerment needs to combine understanding with inspiration, stronger feelings of self-efficacy and fulfillment. In their book *Switch: How to Change Things When Change Is Hard,* Chip and Dan Heath demonstrate that knowledge and willpower are not enough to create meaningful change.[20] Neither is emotion nor is changing the material circumstances in which decisions are made. Lasting change is easier to accomplish when all three components are aligned.

The Heaths call this combination the rider, the elephant, and the path. The rider refers to reason, the part of us that decides where to go. The rider might be able to exert some willpower for a short time but, as everyone knows from experience, willpower is quickly exhausted and the effort to create change grinds to a halt. The failure of New Year's resolutions and strict diets proves the point. The rider can do better by appealing to the motivating power of emotion, which is the elephant. The elephant is a good metaphor for emotional drive because of its great strength and enduring power.

Emotion needs to be directed, however, or it can be destructive. In Laurence Gonzales' studies of the survival scenarios, those who are unable to harness and direct their emotions tend to flail and make poor decisions. Exhausted and confused, they eventually spiral downhill. Few of these people survive.[21]

Research evidence suggests that, when it comes to climate change, worry is a more useful emotion than fear. Whereas fear is often paralyzing, people are eager to resolve the issues that make them worried. Hope is also powerfully motivating, and the combination of worry and hope is better still.[22]

Anger has been a featured emotion in campaigns that target polluters for a wide variety of environmental and public health issues. The efficacy of inspiring anger toward companies that have profited from global warming at the expense of everyone else, however, might be more nuanced. Global warming is often framed as the consequence of everyone's behavior rather than the actions of a few companies that have knowingly resisted policy changes that would reduce their profits. Communication researchers advise caution until this issue is better understood:

> There is strong evidence that anger about corruption and deception comes easily to Americans, including those who are dismissive about global warming. However, there is also good evidence that people resist a framing that implies that they, themselves, have been duped as a result of this corruption.[23]

The motivating power of worry and hope, then, combined with the directive to stop using fossil fuels as quickly as possible provides two of the three elements needed to effect change. The third element is the path, which must be cleared of obstacles. Even a highly motivated elephant can be blocked by a wall that is large enough or a bridge that has fallen down. There is, for example, no value in shaming people for behaviors that they cannot avoid. What are drivers supposed to do if there are no sidewalks, no bicycle lanes and no bus service? Those who feel shamed when they have no reasonable alternatives are likely to become dismissive and resentful. The goal, remember, is to make people feel better, not worse.

Providing new options might be as complicated as redesigning a city's transportation system or as simple as allowing more people to work from home. The thing to remember is that the material circumstances are just as important as the sense of direction and the desire people feel to get there.

Clearing the path can also work in cultural ways. As noted earlier, when I spoke to fellow business owners about my personal motivations for reducing carbon pollution, one of them said, "I can't tell you how good it feels to finally be in a business meeting where I can talk about things I really care about." He was expressing the fact that, in business meetings, talking about personal convictions and the climate crisis is taboo. I recall saying, at the time, that mentioning global warming in a party is an excellent way to end a conversation. Taboos and inhibitions are real obstacles and clearing them away is important too.

Break the Ice

According to a recent survey, only about one-third of the public in the United States talks "often" or "occasionally" about climate change with their family and friends. Two-thirds say they "rarely" or "never" discuss the issue. The reasons vary, from saying that the issue never comes up in conversation to concerns that the issue is too political. Some people say that talking about global warming has never even occurred to them.[24]

Encouraging more climate talk in a variety of different situations and in ways that make people feel inspired and empowered can break the ice and make responding to the crisis seem more mainstream. As Gould suggests,

Help us change each other. The fuel of social change is horizontal, not vertical, influence. As the rise of social media makes clear, people don't respond to the powers that be, they respond to each other. Arm them with relevant content to share and signals to display. It's the secret of generating awareness, setting new agendas for policymakers and creating new social norms.[25]

This advice helps overcome the widespread but incorrect belief that people cannot change. As Gould puts it:

> Any sentence that ends "because that's just how they are" defies sixty years of psychological research that tells us otherwise. We are constantly changing in response to the world and the people around us. We don't need to change human nature. We need to harness our understanding of it.[26]

All of this advice suggests that creating a culture of climate empowerment can be an inspiring, upbeat and joyous experience. People will still argue and disagree, of course, especially in such a polarized society. But the rancor can also be a distraction; giving it too much power is self-defeating. The time has come to lift the dreary veil on the climate crisis and celebrate the power people actually have to reinvent their own lives, their communities, and the world.

Take a Psychological Step

There is one last piece to consider, as well, and that is to embrace the power of making people cross a line in the sand. Advertisers understand how powerful it is to get a demonstration of commitment from customers. The commitment does not need to be big, but it does need to be meaningful. When people make commitments, especially to themselves, they feel obligated to follow through.

Scientists and science educators might balk at a suggestion that seems so manipulative, but, in fact, educators employ this strategy all the time. In museums, for example, exhibits that allow people to use their own hands to interact with information are considered to offer greater educational value than passive experiences. Hands-on exhibits ask people to do something meaningful—to cross a line in the sand—by pressing a button or turning a crank. Crossing this psychological line expresses a commitment to learn something new.

There is nothing coercive or manipulative about offering hands-on learning opportunities to museum goers, but the psychological processes are the same as those used by marketing organizations to boost sales. Educators, advertisers, scientists and social change advocates have different goals and agendas. Some of these goals are highly manipulative. Others are aimed at informing and empowering people to make decisions on their own behalf. The underlying psychology of human beings, combined with the competitive environment in which all communication takes place, makes these different agendas and the interplay between them endlessly fascinating and useful to understand.

Chapter 5

Climate Justice and a White Male

Wealthy people and nations enjoy most of the benefits of fossil energy while poorer people and nations, especially in the Global South, suffer disproportionately from the harmful consequences. Global warming has, in fact, already been harming poor people and people of color for a very long time.[1] The evidence is overwhelming that they suffer the most from air and water pollution, heat stress, hunger, displacement, unemployment and violence.

These facts are well understood in climate circles. Perhaps public understanding is catching up. The horrific murders of George Floyd, Breonna Taylor, Rayshard Brooks and other African Americans in 2020, and the Black Lives Matter protests that quickly followed made systemic inequities clearer than ever to people in the United States. Black, Indigenous, and other people of color live significantly more dangerous lives, in poorer health and with fewer opportunities. They also suffer more exposure to COVID-19 than do whites, and they are dying at much higher rates.[2]

A survey in June of 2020 found that a majority of Americans support the Black Lives Matter movement, partisan differences notwithstanding.[3] Politicians took notice too. The U.S. House of Representatives' *Solving the Climate Crisis* report declares that action on climate change provides a pathway to recover from the pandemic and the resulting economic crisis and to "begin to repair the legacy of environmental pollution that has burdened low-income communities and communities of color for decades. Climate solutions must have justice and equity at their core."[4]

People who live in historically marginalized communities have a lot to say about getting climate solutions right. A report in the *Washington Post* described how predominantly Black and Latino neighborhoods in Phoenix, Arizona, are devoid of shade and, consequently, much hotter than wealthier, predominantly white parts of the city. Rising temperatures in Phoenix are quickly making these low-income neighborhoods unsafe. Just walking home from the bus stop puts people's health at risk on very hot days. Through a process that seems all too rare in local governance, city leaders engaged with the local residents to learn where the best places would be to create new shade. Local knowledge made a significant difference and directed investments to places where they can do the most good.[5] Local knowledge is, in fact, an invaluable asset for advancing climate stability, justice and resilient communities that can withstand a warming world.

From a public empowerment perspective, Joseph Campbell's description of the hero's journey is useful. The hero is someone who perseveres through adversity and whose eventual triumph brings something of great value to the community. Who are the heroes of this story about Phoenix? An answer that reflects traditional power dynamics might focus on the city planners. They engaged with the community in a productive way and used tax dollars efficiently. They are not the heroes, though, because their role was to assist. The real heroes are the members of the local neighborhoods whose knowledge, efforts and guidance made life better.

Being able to identify who the heroes really are is crucial. Scientists, communication practitioners, educators, policymakers and so many others whom we think of as leaders are the assistants. The key actors are the members of our communities who actually create positive change. They are the heroes in Campbell's sense of the term because they are the ones who must overcome adversity to create value. We would be wise to think of the people who are on the front lines of the climate crisis, meaning historically marginalized peoples, as the heroes who can transform their communities.

Celebrating these people and what they accomplish, is one of the best ways to increase everyone's sense of self-efficacy. Scientists and policymakers are the assistants. Why, then, do so many high-level discussions about climate solutions take place exclusively among those who assist? Why are Campbell's heroes—the people who are suffering the most and whose insights can create positive change—absent? When you hear, for example, a debate about investing in carbon capture and storage technologies in order to extend the useful life of fossil fuels, do you wonder why the people who live downwind from powerplants and along congested freeways are not participating? Did they already volunteer to suffer higher rates of childhood asthma and respiratory disease, miss more days of work and school and spend more time in emergency rooms? Did these people, whose rights and interests have been marginalized for so long, actually agree to step up and take one for the team? Not likely. Climate action that is based on injustice will, inevitably, perpetuate injustice.

It has been said that in 2020, white people need to have their own conversations about race. I agree. I once lived in central Los Angeles, where white people like me were in the minority. Nobody who lived there seemed to have much money and almost nobody had air conditioning. During the 1980s, the summers in Los Angeles were relentless. The air was stagnant, smoggy and brutally hot. I was aware at the time that being white and well educated gave me the means to work my way out if I chose to. I knew that most of my neighbors did not have that option. I cannot, therefore, speak to the experiences of my neighbors in low-income, multi-ethnic Los Angeles or anywhere else. I only have enough common experience to empathize. But I can talk about the relief I felt knowing I'd be able to move out someday, and I can speak to the discomfort that comes with that privilege and with ignoring that this reality persists.

With this in mind let's start talking, badly and imperfectly, about climate justice and systemic and unintended racism. Why, for example, isn't climate justice the central focus of most conferences, forums, town halls, listening sessions, workshops, public lectures and creative projects about the climate crisis? Why do so many of us look around these events and see mostly white faces? Why do so many conversations about environmental issues seem to occur in different locations and at different times than conversations about environmental justice? Why, in the racially diverse city where I live, does a network of sustainability-minded local businesses find it so difficult to diversify its membership? And to what extent might I simply be traveling in the wrong circles?

I can think of two possible answers. They are just hypotheses, and I admit up front that they might be wrong. One answer will sound descriptive and fairly benign on its surface, while the other is more uncomfortable to confront. If we are going to hang the climate crisis upside down, though, we are going to expose flaws in our assumptions and perceptions, so discomfort comes with the territory.

The first answer has to do with the culture of science. Science is under siege in the United States, and no aspect of science has been attacked more viciously and consistently than climate science.

Imagine, for a moment, that you are a mild-mannered climate researcher working in a respected university. You and your team of collaborators make a discovery that puts global warming in a historical context. You subject your findings to the scrutiny of your peers by submitting them to a scientific journal. Almost as an afterthought, you decide to include a graph of that historical context. The graph is not the main point of your report, but its hockey-stick shape captures all the attention.

Before long, you find yourself being compared to a convicted rapist and child abuser by right-wing media outlets. You and your department are besieged by demands to release your data, not for honest peer review but to overwhelm and punish you while conducting opposition research. You arrive for work one day to find police tape stretched across your office door because an envelope arrived in the mail containing a white powder. The Anthrax scare is underway, so they won't let you in. And Ken Cuccinelli, then the Virginia Attorney General, uses the full authority of state government to harass you. He seeks a broad range of documents in court under the 2002 Virginia Fraud Against Taxpayers Act because some of your research was once funded by taxpayer dollars.

These things actually happened to a climate scientist named Michael Mann. Cuccinelli's efforts ultimately failed and numerous other studies confirmed the findings that Dr. Mann and his colleagues published. [6] Efforts to harass and discredit Mann and other scientists, however, have been so onerous and relentless that they led to the formation of the Climate Science Legal Defense Fund. It is worth asking why such a fund would ever be necessary.

Michael Mann's story demonstrates how aggressively fossil fuel companies and ideologically conservative organizations have targeted the science they dislike. My guess is that these experiences have heightened long-established sensitivities about defending and protecting the reputation of science as a public good. Except for the people we know personally, climate scientists are the most trusted sources for information about climate change. [7] We trust scientists because they work so hard to present their work as objectively as they can, including being clear about the limitations of their knowledge. Attacking the integrity of science, and of climate scientists in particular, is really a public relations strategy. The goal is to sway public opinion.

One of the ways in which science institutions protect their reputations is by keeping activists at arm's length. Science is about the dispassionate presentation of evidence so that policymakers and citizens can weigh it alongside other priorities and make informed choices. Scientists do not advocate for particular policies in the course of doing their work. The environmental justice movement, on the other hand, is about advocacy: advocacy for equitable representation, relief from the harmful effects of pollution and climate change, and equal access to opportunities.

Does this mean that scientists don't care about climate justice? No, but no matter how passionately individual scientists might feel about the issue, one way or another, they understand that science serves society best by providing honest evidence about the conditions in which people are living today and how those conditions are likely to change in the future.

The COVID-19 crisis has already shown how dangerous it is to politicize science. By sidelining the Centers for Disease Control and Prevention (CDC), which is arguably the premier public health agency in the world, and promoting unproven therapies such as hydroxychloroquine, the Trump administration sowed confusion and undermined confidence in the results of medical science. The administration's attacks on the CDC and Dr. Anthony Fauci, in particular, are part of the same public relations strategy that was used against Dr. Mann and other climate researchers.

Discrediting scientists creates confusion and distrust. In the case of COVID-19 we could see the results in the summer of 2020: fewer people were distancing and wearing masks, and case numbers rose. The harmful effects of climate change are increasing, too, as people and societies fail to unite and focus on reducing and eliminating carbon pollution.

When James Hansen, the famous NASA climatologist who first warned Congress about global warming in 1988, was arrested for protesting at a West Virginia coal plant in 2009,[8] I received a call from a reporter. She said she was doing a story about whether Dr. Hansen was still relevant. Those are the words she used. We are talking about one of the most authoritative experts on the climate system, but his crossing the line into advocacy called his record and his future into question.

Scientific reticence about advocacy is sometimes even more explicit. More than one scientist has told me that they advise their younger colleagues not to speak out about climate change until after they have earned tenure. In other words, getting too close to advocacy could jeopardize a young scientist's career. I have seen this up close too. I was once warned by a scientific institution that if I became known for climate advocacy, they would never be able to work with me again.

The attacks on Michael Mann and other scientists, the warnings to young scientists and communicators like me, and the implicit criticism of James Hansen are signs that public trust in science is under attack. The fact that Dr. Fauci and the CDC got the same treatment suggests that we can expect to see more of this public relations strategy in the future. Let's recognize the harassment for what it is.

I can understand why the science community is cautious about advocacy and advocates, yet extreme caution also has consequences. The careful and dispassionate emotional tone used in scientific presentations can make people question how urgent the crisis really is. Science historian Naomi Oreskes, co-author of *Merchants of Doubt*, once described how a schoolteacher admonished a panel of climate scientists by saying, "You guys are telling us about all these incredibly grave consequences that we are facing, but not one of you sounds like you're actually worried." She went on to characterize the scientists' reluctance to say anything stronger this way: "We don't speak in the emotional register that's appropriate for this concern because, if we do, we're afraid that we'll be discredited."[9]

Herein lies one of the structural ways in which the voices of environmental justice advocates are pushed out of the mainstream. As Oreskes put it, "it's important for the scientific community to recognize that the pressure on scientists not to be advocates is actually part of the disinformation campaign."

Think about that: climate deniers are using the culture of science itself to undermine scientists who speak out about the urgency that their evidence reveals. Where science should go from here is a matter of ongoing and sometimes intense debate. There is little agreement about whether speaking as passionate advocates would have a positive or negative impact on the public. Unfortunately, there is very little research evidence to go on.

Given that we are talking about climate justice, do you find this answer satisfying? It is accurate, but is it sufficient? I think not, as Senator Cory Booker made clear when he read the following paragraph by author James Baldwin during a discussion of racial justice in July of 2020.[10] Baldwin wrote,

I'm talking about what happens to you if, having barely escaped suicide, or death, or madness, or yourself, you watch your children growing up and no matter what you do, no matter what you do, you are powerless, you are really powerless, against the force of the world that is out to tell your child that he has no right to be alive. And no amount of liberal jargon, and no amount of talk about how well and how far we have progressed, does anything to soften or to point out any solution to this dilemma. In every generation, ever since Negroes have been here, every Negro mother and father has had to face that child and try to create in that child some way of surviving this particular world, some way to make the child who will be despised not despise himself. I don't know what "the Negro problem" means to white people, but this is what it means to Negroes.[11]

As Naomi Oreskes says, much of the discussion about climate change does not occur in an emotional register that is appropriate;

not to pain like this. Nor does it fully explain why white people with good intentions, who believe strongly that everyone is equal and should be treated as such, think and behave in ways that allow systemic racism and the marginalization of Indigenous peoples to persist. We need to look further and deeper. When we do, I think we begin to see some of the ways in which we—meaning white people like me—learn to discount and marginalize opinions, judgments, knowledge and experiences when we hear them expressed by people of color.

We are wired to perpetuate the past without thinking very much about it. I don't say this to excuse anything. That would be dismissive of something that is truly important. I mention it because these habits are real, and they need to be disrupted in order for us to overcome them.

Because these processes are learned, we need to acknowledge our own lived experiences. During the 1980s, for example, I worked frequently with woodworkers who were white and male. Theirs was a culture of constant probing and testing to see who would fit in, who would not and who would emerge as the alpha male. If, for example, a new employee showed up on the first day with a brand new toolbelt, the hazing and teasing would last for years. This was also a culture of extremely vivid and overtly racist and sexist language. The words were used in a matter-of-fact way and as jokes and as ways to challenge people to see where they stood. Objecting to such language led to repeated challenges, and sometimes I found it easier just to ignore it. Since I needed to work with these people, I wrestled with which battles to pick. For whatever reason, things changed in the 1990s. The girlie tool calendars vanished from the walls and the opened lids of toolboxes. The language was cleaned up, too, as the labor force gradually began to look more Hispanic.

Have you had your own version of these experiences? Did the underlying racism end when the language changed? Of course not. I hoped that it had, but I was also relieved not to have to deal with it anymore. The horrific events of 2020 revealed the truth: society had not changed. Our mental models and unconscious behavioral scripts are still at odds with the realities that people of color are living.

I think that many white people, me included, feel this disconnect. There is psychic discomfort when a belief (I am not a racist), a mental model (everybody is inherently equal) and unconscious scripts (I must be doing something right) run into conflict with hard evidence to the contrary. The cognitive dissonance is jarring, and I think it leads to some awkward failures: it's not me (so I don't have to deal with it), it is me (and I don't know how to fix it), I try to fix it (and activists of color don't want to engage with me), and I want this anxiety to end (I feel guilty, so I make a big show of how much I care). These are failures because they avoid the genuine contact and conversation that can rewrite the scripts.

We are acculturated to marginalize people of color and treat the climate justice movement as something separate. Each one of us grows up under the guidance of teachers and mentors. Our advancement in education and careers, and in our social standing, largely depends on our ability to meet the standards and join the culture of those mentors. Advancement is only partly achieved by doing good work. Some of it probably comes by change, but a large portion, if not the largest share, comes from the support of those who have the power to help us if we measure up. There are times, of course, when standing up to the powers that be can help us advance, but these are exceptional circumstances. We advance through acculturation, by learning the language and standards of the gatekeepers.

At the same time, we learn to diminish the opinions of other people who do not speak the same language and whose approaches, messages, affect and style don't seem to fit in. There is wiggle room of course, more in some environments than in others, but marginalizing people who seem less powerful, less wealthy, less educated, less knowledgeable and less refined—according to accepted standards—is one of the norms. It is about who fits in and who does not. We are not talking about substance here. We are talking about accents, mannerisms, skin color, clothing and other codes around which our unconscious behavior revolves. As we internalize the norms—as we simplify inappropriately—we adopt behaviors that dismiss other people without giving it much thought.

This is one of the ways in which systemic racism persists. The process is situational, meaning that it might not apply to people of color whom we know personally or who have attained high stature. Its connection to policymaking might not be entirely obvious. But the largely unconscious processes that lead us to give greater weight to certain ideas based on where they come from is one of the reasons why policies that perpetuate racial injustice are so resistant to change. As noted earlier, humans defend status quo, and the status quo was established by white people.

I was most conscious of this dynamic when I was getting into my career. I could often tell when someone who had power was checking me out. The behavior of those carpenters was blatant, but I experienced a more subtle version of the same thing from corporate leadership. Academia and the sciences felt different, but by how much? There is still a huge gender gap in the sciences. So, have I eliminated my acculturation? Have you? If we had, I doubt society would be what it is today. Like the scripts that led people to laugh as the tsunami wave gathered around their ankles and started to rise, these scripts need to be washed away and rewritten. We might not mean to think this way. I certainly don't, but just like every other human being, I simplify. Simplifying is an inescapable process, and just like everyone else, I simplify in biased and inappropriate ways. I learned those biases through social interactions, in the same ways everybody else did. As a result, systemic racism is still with us, in spite of our desires and better judgment.

These comments are not meant as self-soothing self-help. We are talking about decarbonizing the global economy and improving our health and wellbeing in the process. We are talking about who has the power to be heard, the standards by which decisions are made and who is making the decisions in the first place. As the majority in the U.S. House of Representatives declared, political action for climate justice is inseparable from solving the climate crisis itself. Decision-making power needs to represent the people, not our unconscious habits.

Some might say, correctly, that the public in the United States is divided on race relations. Support for Black Lives Matter is not universal, and the House report was written by the Democratic majority. So the question arises whether I am arguing for a political agenda. This question, just like those that pressure scientists never to speak out forcefully, is actually a feature of the disinformation campaign. The underlying strategy is to discredit anyone who speaks up.

Let's look at the question in practical terms. How did anti-scientific, laissez-faire responses to the coronavirus pandemic play out? Physical distancing was almost universal in March of 2020, but the unity broke down in places where health guidelines were relaxed. Infections skyrocketed in those places. Suppressing the epidemic depends on most people acting for the same common good. Likewise, overcoming the climate crisis depends on widespread participation. Does it make sense to exclude or ignore large groups of people? Would there be any efficacy or justice in doing so? How, after all, can a society with such deep racial and class inequities hope to survive the compounding pressures that the changing climate is already starting to impose?

We depend on the collective agency and insights of our communities, not merely those who happen to be the powers that be. Our assignment therefore is to release the grip on power, genuinely engage, listen and adapt. Do not expect to be met halfway with open arms. That would be entirely unrealistic. Those who have been victimized and excluded from power for generations have good reason to be distrustful. As Gonzales explains, building trust is about rewriting our learned and unconscious scripts:

> The central task for the emotional system is to classify the consequences of our behavior in the world, so the natural conclusion the organism draws is that we're doing something right. If we're getting fed every day, our strategy must be a good one, so we don't even have to think about it. We can simply continue doing what we've always done. Life is good. Our little corner of the world is safe. But life wasn't always like that. It still isn't for many people in the world. The emotional systems that those people build up are very different from ours.[12]

The emotional systems of privileged people draw the conclusion that we are doing something right. We should be suspicious of this conclusion. People who have been marginalized have built up emotional systems that reach very different conclusions. As James Baldwin wrote, they are trained to be wary, based on a history of oppression, unkept promises, hostility and violence.

The assignment for white people is to release power—real authority—to those who have been marginalized in the past. This might feel unsettling because our emotional systems have learned to be comfortable with the status quo. But it is impossible to protect the status quo and make progress at the same time. This is what climate justice, environmental justice more broadly, and the adaptive approach to solving this global crisis require of us. Discomfort comes with the territory until we get used to a new reality when we will trust, once again, that we must be doing something right. Building mutual trust between the oppressors and the oppressed—regardless of how self-consciously or unconsciously the oppression is delivered—takes time and genuine contact. And, it will definitely be worthwhile.

Perhaps shifting power in this way is a stretch goal too: *Genuinely engage and quickly empower historically marginalized people and absolutely, positively do not fail.*

Fortunately, this goal is as clear as our other stretch goal. How do we get this done? Elect more candidates of color to pubic office? Select messengers for communication campaigns who speak authentically for their communities? Create meaningful space in climate conferences and decision-making processes for authentic voices to guide and lead? Remember the advice given in the previous chapter: genuinely connect. This requires the kind of dialog that gets past simple transactions and traditional power dynamics in order to build understanding and trust. The next chapter will describe how we might advance this part of the work in a very powerful way.

Chapter 6

A Plan to Turn Things Around

In the preceding chapters I described a few of the many organizations, initiatives and people who are moving society closer to a culture of empowerment. If their examples struck you as curious anecdotes rather than pieces of a coherent program, you would be right. There is no master plan to shift our culture into action or do the genuine engagement that will help us overcome structural racism.

But the people who are doing this work touch every corner of society, from community organizing to environmental justice, science education, science communication, communication research, media relations, advertising, social marketing, policy development, professional and technical training, entrepreneurship and innovation in just about every field you can imagine. These people understand the climate crisis. They come from diverse backgrounds and, in the United States, they come from all over the world. While many of these people exchange ideas and knowledge from time to time, there is a genuine hunger for greater strategic alignment.

When a group of communication researchers and practitioners gathered in 2015, for example, they called for an increased community-wide strategic planning capability. Noting the diffused manner in which people and organizations work, they acknowledged remarkable successes, especially in the face of the nationwide disinformation campaign, while also agreeing that the accomplishments have not yet been sufficient.[1]

Consider the competitive imbalance between these diffused efforts and the initiatives designed to misinform the public and dissuade people from taking action. Funded and organized largely by fossil fuel companies, including Exxon Mobil, Chevron,

Valero and others, along with wealthy individuals including Charles and the late David Koch, the denial campaign supports a network of think tanks, issues misleading pseudo-scientific reports, drafts sample legislation, files lawsuits, calls the integrity of the scientific enterprise into question and stokes suspicion that climate change is really a disguise for an anti-free market political agenda. Despite repeated exposure in the national media, these efforts appear to be ongoing. In June 2020, for example, during the nationwide Black Lives Matter protests, the *E&E* news service reported that Chevron had hired a Virginia-based communication firm. The assignment was to urge journalists to write stories about how green groups were promoting policies that would hurt minority communities. *E&E* summarized the initiative this way:

"It was an audacious messaging campaign: White environmentalists are hurting black communities by pushing radical climate policies that would strip them of fossil fuel jobs."[2]

On the other side, funds for public engagement are invested without overall planning. Support falls into two broad categories. In one category, federal dollars fund grant competitions from time to time. The money supports education and outreach pilot projects, which means funding is short term and the projects are relatively small. Philanthropy is the other category and it supports some of the more established outreach organizations over longer periods of time. New expenditures, however, tend to fund the philanthropists' in-house priorities and are constrained by institutional guidelines. As a result, few of these investments reach their full strategic potential, and very few successful initiatives are able to grow in scale.

As a case in point, I participated in an educational advertising campaign about climate science in 2012-14 for which the principal investigators received White House Champions of Change recognition. This was a high honor, and it demonstrated that the campaign impressed some high-ranking people. Our strategy was to use advertising in mass transit cars and stations to accomplish three things: increase confidence in climate science during phase one, increase a sense of local relevance in phase two, and build hope by identifying local climate leaders during phase three. The campaign was, indeed, highly successful in building awareness. Surveys showed that the ads created the most recognized brand ever to appear in the city's transit advertising. Does this mean the campaign changed people's minds? We have good reasons to think so, but, unfortunately, we will never know for sure. The campaign was designed around research evidence showing the types of messages that should work, and the ads tested well in focus groups. Once the campaign was in the field, however, evaluators found it impossible to determine the campaign's impact because just about everybody saw the ads. There was no control group. After winning its award, the campaign was archived and never exported to other cities because the principal investigators were unable to find financial backing. The humorous ads, which feature a flock of irascible ostriches coming to terms with the climate crisis can still be seen at ScienceToGo.org.

The point is that we can do better. Investments in outreach projects can and should be grounded in better measurement and evaluation. Programs that work can and should be expanded in order to engage with more people. And decisions about which ideas deserve funding in the first place can be made in more disciplined ways with greater strategic alignment.

The Paris Agreement and the underlying United Nations Convention on Climate Change (UNFCCC) recognize the importance of improving public engagement in this way:

The solutions to the negative effects of climate change are also the paths to a safer, healthier, cleaner and more prosperous future for all. However, for such a future to become reality, citizens of all countries, at all levels of government, society and enterprise, need to understand and be involved.[3]

The UN's name for public engagement is "Action for Climate Empowerment" (ACE). According to UNFCCC Article 6 and Article 12 of the Paris Agreement, ACE efforts need to embrace inclusive decision-making processes that are sensitive to gender, intergenerational, Indigenous and racial concerns. Climate justice is integral to the international community's agreement to tackle the climate crisis. These values are encouraged, moreover, in language that amounts to a concrete obligation. Each nation that is part of the UNFCCC and the Paris Agreement is supposed to designate a national focal point for ACE activities and develop a national strategy that follows UN guidelines. In other words, nations are expected to create and report on national strategic plans for increasing public participation, empowerment and understanding.[4]

Before turning to what an ACE national strategic plan might look like in the United States, take a moment to imagine what strategic planning can accomplish. A plan will guide increased and sustained investments in ACE activities, which is extremely important. Community organizers describe how the grant application process is often so onerous that they cannot compete. Grants tend to support the newest, sexiest concepts, but not the infrastructure and salaries that allow change agents to stay involved and develop their programs.

A strategic plan can encourage greater collaboration across the many ACE disciplines. As Baruch Fischhoff observed in 2007,

Climate science is needed to focus on choices that matter and get the facts right. Decision science is needed to identify the facts that should matter most when people evaluate their options. Social science is needed to describe people's perceptions of those critical facts, as well as their goals when making choices.[5]

Writers and designers are also needed to make the information appealing and sticky. Eight years later, Fischhoff described how strategic collaborations can also help the ACE community overcome some of its own biases:

> Natural scientists will need to respect the social sciences, not just assume that more evidence will win the day. Social scientists will need to draw on all relevant results, not just their own specialty. Climate activists will need to test their communications, not just trust their hunches about what people need to hear.[6]

One of the most significant gaps that I have seen recently is an urgent need to train city leaders in strategic communication. So much of the climate policy and behavior change work revolves around municipal policies, planning and local interactions with utility companies, local businesses, community groups and families. Very few cities can afford to hire communication agencies to develop messaging campaigns. Everything must be done inhouse by people who, typically, have no communication expertise. This gap represents an opportunity to scale up the training work that informal networks are already doing and rapidly build capacity where it is needed most.

This is just the tip of the proverbial iceberg. A national strategic plan for ACE will also provide inclusive mechanisms to exchange knowledge and marshal the amazing work that is being accomplished in communities and neighborhoods everywhere. A plan can guide evidence-based messaging strategies that inspire greater confidence and hope. Practitioners can increase their own sense of efficacy by understanding who their natural allies are and how their efforts fit into an overall framework. From a political perspective, a national strategic plan will make the all-important cultural shift a national priority, help guide and support frontline work in cities and rural areas and, potentially, assert international leadership on the climate issue.

At the same time, an ongoing strategic planning process can impose a crucial type of discipline on the work that everyone is doing. When the sense of urgency is high, people feel compelled to charge into action as fast as they can. Action feels better than inaction. Moving too quickly, however, pushes everyone into transactional relationships and decision-making at the expense of the genuine conversations that are so urgently needed. Building climate justice into climate action requires that people slow down and let the conversations work their magic. In his book, *The Magic of Dialogue,* Daniel Yankelovich puts his finger on the key point:

> In traditional hierarchical arrangements, those at the top of the pecking order can afford to be casual about how well they understand those at lower levels. When people are more equal, they are obligated to make a greater effort to understand each other. If no one is the undisputed boss anymore, and if all insist on having their views respected, it follows that people *must* understand each other. You don't really have a voice if those making the decisions aren't prepared to listen to you.[7]

If overcoming long-stand habits that marginalize blacks, Indigenous people and other people of color is truly inseparable from solving the climate crisis, then we need more dialog. We need to set fast-paced transactional relationships and power hierarchies aside for enough time to learn each other's values, assumptions and aspirations. This is the process that builds mutual understanding and trust.

International Guidelines for Empowerment

International negotiators created the Action for Climate Empowerment agenda in an interesting way that encourages people to step outside of the traditional boundaries between education, communication, community organizing and the social sciences. They define six different elements of ACE, along with a set of objectives that intentionally defy easy categorization. The ACE elements, in fact, force people to engage with others who approach the challenges from different directions. As a consequence, the entire structure might look messy, but only at first glance.

The six elements are described as follows.

1. *Education* "enables people to understand the causes and consequences of climate change" [8] and make informed decisions accordingly. Education activities take place in formal schooling from the elementary through post-graduate study, and in a variety of informal settings that include museums, aquariums, zoos, cultural centers and so forth. Documentary films and journalism play a role in public education, as do public service announcements, official reports and a host of other activities that might not come to mind when you think of education.

2. *Training* speaks to building the technical, professional and practical skills that people can put into practice immediately. Whereas education typically operates on longer time horizons, training is about building capacity quickly. Here, again, the range is enormous, from gathering and interpreting data about emissions, public health and the climate system to technical skills in infrastructure management, agricultural and forestry practices, supply chain management, urban planning, emergency response and countless other fields. Skills training is also needed to help community organizing and environmental justice programs expand and to help governments learn new ways to give them resources and power. New knowledge emerges quickly, so disseminating information and best practices is an ongoing priority.

Together, education and training target public understanding of the changing climate and build capacity to address its effects. The next two elements focus on improving community engagement, experimentation and knowledge development in order to find and promote climate solutions.

3. *Public awareness* is where the emphasis shifts to strategic communication that literally changes behavior. The guidelines require nations to

> Assess needs specific to national circumstances ... using special research methods and other relevant instruments to determine target audiences and potential partnerships; and develop communication strategies on climate change based on targeted social research in order to create behavioural changes.[9]

This is where the UNFCCC recognizes the full range of psychological and social factors that influence the choices people make. Communication researchers, behavioral scientists, advertisers and social marketers are obvious candidates for this work. But nonprofit organizations, utility companies, health organizations and others who promote the adoption of beneficial behaviors belong here too.

4. *Public access to information* refers to climate information, statistics and other data. The rationale behind this element is that free access to information "is crucial in order to develop and implement effective policies and to engage people actively in implementing these policies."[10] The agenda goes much deeper, however, as it "strengthens connections between knowledge production, knowledge sharing, and decision-making, and provides people with the tools they need to play an active role in addressing climate change."[11] We are talking about everything from national databases to citizen science, community-level learning, knowledge and ways of knowing within Indigenous

communities, knowledge generated by businesses and more. Some aspects of this element are technocratic, while others involve fostering human interactions and storytelling. If you watched any of the short videos posted by ICU nurses who were working with COVID patients, for example, you have experienced storytelling as a powerful gateway to information.

5. *Public participation* is the fifth element. It speaks to "ownership by encouraging people to be more attentive to policy-making and participate in the implementation of climate policies."[12] The focus is on removing the barriers that limit public participation in civic life at the local, regional and national levels. The UNFCCC recognizes that "In some places, this will prompt profound changes in how political leaders and civil servants are accustomed to working and encourage people to be more attentive to policy-making."[13] Many of us are accustomed to thinking about civic participation as either voting or joining activist groups, but the agenda is much broader. The ACE strategy calls on governments to find new ways to engage with the public and actively remove barriers that tend to limit participation to only the special interests and the most highly motivated advocates.

Several models for encouraging public participation already exist in the United States. Protests, including camping out in legislators' offices, are probably the easiest to recognize, but civic leaders often engage in other ways as well. Perhaps you have participated in some of the public discussions and listening sessions about important issues in your community. Perhaps you have engaged with officials from various government agencies about rulemaking or utilized some of the resources they offer to make the work you do more productive. The goal of the ACE public participation element is to do more of these things and do them with a much greater focus on reducing global warming and improving community resilience.

6. International cooperation. The final element is a cross-cutting agenda that strengthens all of the others. Governments are expected to share knowledge, ideas and technical expertise in order to help the international community accelerate a just transition to a low-carbon world. Here, too, the ACE elements break down traditional silos because governments cannot fulfill this agenda entirely on their own. Businesses, nongovernmental organizations, trade associations, professional societies and a range of other ACE actors are equally important because the main objective of elements five and six is to foster debate and partnerships that engage all stakeholders in a collective response to the climate crisis.

I mentioned that the ACE elements might look somewhat messy at the outset. If we hang the mental map upside down, however, the wisdom of this approach reveals itself. The strategic planning process in each country leads people into new associations and provides them with new goals. From this perspective, the six elements of ACE have the same effect as stretch goals in that they force everyone to look at their work in new ways. The overarching goal is still very simple: empower the public and their governments to reduce global warming and build more resilient communities. The procedures by which this can happen encourage people to work together, share knowledge, increase dialog and form lasting partnerships with a wider range of people.

No single consulting firm or government agency can put a national strategy of this type together on its own. Even though a small team of people will coordinate the effort and write the final plan, ACE guidelines require them to build inclusive processes into the planning so that the voices of experienced ACE practitioners and historically marginalized communities inform the strategies. Technically speaking, everyone has a vital stake and something of value to contribute. Planners therefore are tasked with finding ways to be inclusive, efficient and concrete at the same time.

In order to facilitate something of this magnitude, the UNFCCC embraces a process called the "2018 Talanoa Dialogue Platform." Talanoa is a Fijian process that is used extensively in the Pacific to "build empathy and to make wise decisions for the collective good."[14] In a Talanoa-style dialog, people are encouraged to set aside combative negotiation agendas and resist the temptation to blame others. Instead, everyone is invited to participate as equals, share stories, listen and, in the process, build more understanding and trust. In a country as large as the United States, implementing this platform to its full potential will take time, yet this is not really a problem. The dialogs need not be finished before a national strategic plan is completed; in fact, the dialog process is meant to expand and become part of the social fabric over the long haul. There is already a corollary to the Talanoa process in the United States. Founded by social scientist Daniel Yankelovich and former Secretary of State Cyrus Vance, a nonprofit organization called Public Agenda builds a similar capacity for sustained and facilitated dialogs in local communities. The ACE guidelines essentially ask nations to increase their capability to do more of this type of work.

An ACE Strategic Plan for the United States

Here's the bad news: As I write this, no major emitting country has submitted an ACE national strategic plan to the UNFCCC. The United States has not yet appointed a national focal point for ACE and, given the Trump Administration's desire to leave the Paris Agreement, they have not launched an official effort to meet this obligation. There is good news, however, because the desire for an inclusive national strategy is so strong across the sprawling ACE community in the United States, that the community itself has undertaken to move forward with the strategic planning agenda unofficially and on its own.

More than two hundred individuals representing nearly

150 different organizations, institutions, tribes and government agencies registered to participate in a series of Talanoa-style dialogs in August of 2020.[15] Following months of planning by a coordination team, on which I serve as a strategic advisor, the dialogs embraced the cross-cutting, multi-sectoral and multi-cultural structure of the ACE guidelines. Individual participants came from universities, such as Yale, Cornell, Columbia, George Mason and others that might be less familiar to you; community groups and social movements including the Citizens' Climate Lobby, WE ACT for Environmental Justice, the Indigenous Environmental Network and El Puente-Latino Climate Action Network and others; tribal governments including the Spokane Tribe of the Spokane Reservation; city governments including those of New York, Orlando, San Luis Obispo and Washington, DC; state and territorial governments such as Puerto Rico and the State of California; consultancies and communication firms such as Fenton and others that are less well known; federal agencies including NOAA, the National Science Foundation and the U.S. Department of State; national and international climate education networks such as the Climate Literacy and Energy Awareness Network, the Climate Education, Communication and Outreach Stakeholders Community and others; think tanks including the Aspen Institute and Brookings Institution; museums and nature centers including the National and New England Aquariums, Aquarium of the Pacific, The Wild Center and Zoo Atlanta; regional planning organizations such as the Capital District Regional Planning Commission; and professional societies such as the American Society of Adaptation Professionals. The participants included members of youth and environmental justice movements, Indigenous movements, climate activists, scientists, educators, researchers, civil servants, elected officials, businesspeople and others. Their contributions proved to be extremely impressive.

Talanoa-style dialogs build mutual understanding, but they

also have concrete planning objectives. Because the participants are professionals who work on public empowerment, their inputs to the dialogs contained useful information about specific opportunities to make their work more effective. As just one example, suggestions were made about reallocating investments so that the duration of funding is better aligned with the objectives of the grants.

You can probably imagine that the dialogs yielded a great deal of material. The next step involves sifting and synthesis, plus careful strategic review. A writing team, which I lead, is responsible for drafting a *U.S. ACE Strategic Planning Framework* that is clear and specific. Recognized leaders in a variety of ACE disciplines and communities, plus the dialog participants themselves, will review the draft and call attention to any significant omissions or errors in nuance. Their feedback will lead to completion of the strategic *Framework* before the end of 2020. A website, https://aceframework.us, is the home of the project and the final product.

The distinction between a framework and a national strategic plan is important because only the executive branch of the federal government can make commitments to the UNFCCC process. Why, then, would so many busy people devote so much time to a voluntary and unsanctioned initiative? This is the question I asked when I was invited to join the coordinating and writing teams. Those of us who work on climate outreach are accustomed to well-intended efforts that build lasting relationships among peers but yield little tangible benefit. What makes this effort different?

I see at least two reasons to make the investment. The first is that the United States is behind on reporting its national contribution to the Paris Agreement process. Periodic "Nationally Determined Contributions" are required from all nations on a strict schedule, and the year 2020 is a milestone. The ACE community therefore sees an opportunity to accelerate development of an ACE national strategy by doing much of the community-building and framing work before the federal government takes up the task. The *Framework* can provide useful guidance whenever a formal planning process begins.

Guidance will be helpful, of course, but what incentive does the federal government have to pay heed to this initiative or, for that matter, develop a national strategy? The short answer is that employees who work at some of the grant-making agencies are participating in the process. This means that the recommendations in the *Framework* speak directly to people who are involved in funding decisions and the design of various outreach programs. The *Framework* will help these people be more responsive to the ACE community's needs. Members of state, tribal and local governments are also involved, so the *Framework's* recommendations about policymaking and community partnerships will help align their decision-making processes as well.

Beyond this, the *Framework,* is a statement of the ACE community's call to action. It urges the federal government to advance the ACE agenda in very specific ways. There is no doubt that the *Framework* will be highly visible to elected officials in the United States and abroad. The hope is that the quality of the final product and the prestige of the contributors will encourage the United States government, philanthropic foundations, professional societies, trade associations and environmental justice and education networks to heed the call and collaborate strategically at long last.

The second reason is that the *Framework* itself will be influential no matter what the future of national politics looks like. I have often thought that the U.S. federal government might be the last institution to take action on the climate crisis because most of the productive work is taking place below the level of national politics. Federal agencies, for example, are actively engaged with their constituencies on specific projects to reduce climate damage ranging from coastal flooding to depletion of commercial fisheries to preventing toxic agricultural runoff into rivers and streams to accelerating the pace of recovery from severe storms. A great deal of this work is grounded in climate science. A number of state governments and multi-state collaborations are reducing energy demand and carbon pollution as well. California, for example, has the most progressive energy efficiency standards in the nation and, as a result, has held per capita electricity use steady since the early 1970s while usage in other states nearly doubled.[16] The City of New York has one of the most thorough climate action plans in the country, and the small farming town of Greensburg, Kansas, is known internationally as a model green city. In total, 290 U.S. cities and counties signed the We Are Still In declaration, which supports the goals of the Paris Agreement. They are joined by some 2,275 businesses and investors, 353 colleges and universities, eighty-four cultural institutions, thirty-two healthcare organizations, fifty-three faith groups, ten states and twelve tribes.[17] For the *U.S. ACE National Strategic Planning Framework,* these are key constituents. Many of them are participating in the *Framework* dialogs and review process, and all of them will benefit from the *Framework's* strategic recommendations.

Conflating the Action for Climate Empowerment agenda with actual reductions in carbon pollution is easy to do. The empowerment agenda, along with its sprawling community of educators, communicators, organizers and funders is aimed at encouraging the public and our elected representatives to take bolder, more confident actions to reduce global warming. This community agrees that "citizens of all countries, at all levels of government, society and enterprise, need to understand and be involved."[18] By joining forces under the guidelines of the Paris Agreement, they also agree that going it alone is not the wisest course of action. They can accomplish more by working together, and they are making a concerted effort to do just that.

Chapter 7

Luckily, It Comes Down to Us

I referenced Laurence Gonzales' studies of catastrophe throughout this book because he describes the features of human psychology that get us stuck in the wicked problem mentality. This mentality keeps us from seeing the climate crisis as a simple problem, full of opportunities to make our lives and communities better. I think Gonzales makes one more important contribution to this discussion as well. It involves leadership.

Like the unfortunate people who stood on the beach in Thailand and watched the tsunami wave roll toward them, not everyone has the experience or perspective to see the climate crisis for what it is. The truth is, people—all people—get so accustomed to seeing things in familiar ways that we miss opportunities to do better. But people are not identical, and some people are better equipped to help us move toward a culture of climate justice and empowerment. The good news is that we are already part of the way there. The majority of U.S. citizens understands that climate change is dangerous and wants our government to do more to reduce the risks.

Waiting for government or anyone else to solve the crisis is not an attribute of empowerment, though, so we have more work to do. Everyone who sees the crisis as our problem to solve has the essential characteristics to be a leader in their family, community and professional life. If this describes you, then you have already turned the corner on the single most important thing any of us can do to reduce global warming.

Does this strike you as an overwhelming burden? If so, Gonzales offers some good advice. He describes the steps that help survivors of real calamities avoid tendencies that lead to despair and make matters worse, such as projection and blaming, passive-aggressive anger, denial, acting out and getting lost in fantasy.[1]

Accepting the reality of the crisis is crucial, of course, and so is noticing the details, especially the details you find humorous. When we did the ad campaign on the Boston metro, we placed ostriches in silly interpretations of very serious climate impacts. Humor gives people enough emotional distance to laugh at their own foibles, which helps them remain calm, get organized, think and make a plan. The next step is to get moving and act on that plan. Active people do not have time to wallow.

If you are unsure what your next steps might be, the appendix to this book is filled with suggestions, initiatives and organizations that you can join. As you take action, remember that it is easy to overlook your successes and only see the work that still lies ahead. The great thing about incremental and adaptive strategies is that they give you plenty of opportunities to celebrate progress. Survivors of extreme disasters celebrate even their smallest accomplishments. While you are at it, count your blessings. Your efforts are meaningful to every living being, so keep at it. As Gonzales writes, "You're still here. That means you can do something."[2]

The COVID-19 crisis is already showing us the way forward. Over the course of just a few days in the middle of March of 2020, the American people and much of the world suddenly stayed home. The skies cleared over U.S. cities and the streets grew quiet. Feelings of anxiety about jobs and infection were palpable and so was a sense of relief at not having to commute and put on our professional costumes. People experienced tragic losses and began to recognize some of the deep inequities that we have taken for granted as those with greater privilege worked from home while those who earn less, and especially people of color, risked their lives to go to work.

We witnessed heroic acts of dedication, courage and self-sacrifice among essential workers, especially in hospitals and clinics. We saw spontaneous acts of generosity and kindness as people found ways to take care of their more vulnerable neighbors. We witnessed outpourings of respect and appreciation on a daily basis in hard-hit New York and when we said "thank you" to the people who checked and bagged our groceries. We saw people celebrating life together even while maintaining physical distance.

Sadly, we also learned how destructive a lack of messaging discipline can be. We watched the U.S. population heed the call to "flatten the curve" and, in many cases, conflate success with having eliminated the virus altogether. We saw how ideologically driven messaging disrupted a nation's sense of common purpose and allowed COVID-19 infections to skyrocket again. As if these tragedies were not enough, the public could not escape seeing horrific police violence against African Americans over and over again.

This curse of a pandemic, however, also gives us a rare moment of opportunity to rethink our situation, shift our expectations and rebuild our lives in ways that we have longed to do. Nobody wants to breathe smog or drink polluted water. Nobody likes to sit in stop-and-go traffic. Nobody enjoys fighting wars to protect oil supply lines. Everybody, it seems, wants to live healthier, more relaxed and rewarding lives.

Giving culture a push—many pushes, in fact—takes strategic thinking and leadership. Leadership, I think, involves overcoming three psychic challenges.

1. Overcoming dread and despair. When you first see the possibility of our stark future you might feel overcome with dread. Gonzales addresses this in the first step toward survival: perceive and believe. Accept the facts, but do not stop there. His twelve steps are, in effect, a different take on the hero's journey. The heroes in the climate story are you, me, our neighbors, those who have been ignored in the past, those from whom we choose to buy products and services and the people who we elect to public office. We are not victims when we take control of our choices.

Those who overcome dread and despair let go of the past and accept the current reality, and they find ways to appreciate the beauty in everyday experiences even in the midst of their predicaments. Most of the people who survive life-or-death calamities overcome despair for the sake of someone else. It could be a loved one, a member of a different species or the human community itself. Either way, making the shift from worrying about oneself to working for the benefit of others is crucial. It turns victims into rescuers, and this makes all the difference. Who, then, matters most to you? Whose future are you willing to work for?

2. *Expanding your boundaries.* As you overcome this first obstacle, you might seek comfort in believing that playing your normal social or professional role is enough. It isn't, of course, unless eliminating carbon pollution is your day job. Finding ways to lead involves accepting a healthy dose of humility and a leap of faith. It involves thinking in ways that put your identity at risk. The decision to go big and to succeed at all costs invokes the psychology of stretch goals. It is a way of setting de facto assumptions aside, of turning the picture upside down to see yourself from a different perspective. That's how you discover your own resources.

3. *Taking ownership.* All of which leads to the third psychic challenge, which is to take ownership of the climate crisis and make solving it your problem, not someone else's. Those of us who are helping people make informed choices about the future and those who make justice their life's work cannot succeed by behaving exactly as we did in the past. Neither can anyone else who wants their loved ones to live in a cleaner, less toxic and more just world.

When you decide that the climate crisis is yours to solve, you discover that the diversity of people's voices and ideas is, in reality, our greatest asset. We will make plenty of mistakes, as humans always do, but it is impossible to foresee which innovations will fail and which will really take off. We can, however, avoid known pitfalls and learn from one another. Marginalizing certain people, their voices and ideas therefore is our greatest weakness. The self-imposed limits that we place on our opportunities through overt and systemic racism and other forms of bigotry have gotten us where we are today. They won't get us out.

We emphasize our limitations when scientists shy away from forceful statements about the breadth of their agreement on the settled science. We limit our potential when we make excuses for dismissing the voices of people who don't look or sound or think the way we do. We limit ourselves when our cultural institutions ignore their visitors' most urgent questions because the answers involve opening the doors to different kinds of expertise. It happens when business leaders avoid speaking forcefully about their real convictions. It happens when faith communities settle for feel-good ministries instead of embracing the moral obligation to lead and call for change. It happens when policymakers give in to industry complaints that transforming our energy system should not involve risks or discomfort. It happens when we draw a line at doing our jobs to the best of our abilities but go no further. It happens, in other words, when we believe our existing assumptions and fail to hang the problem upside down to see it from a fresh perspective.

Does this sound difficult? It is actually quite easy to do, and the experience is exhilarating. Every time you overcome one of these limitations, you will discover that there is a community of good will and shared passion that is eager to welcome new members. This is where opportunity lies.

When you commit to do something and start to take action,

the climate challenge lives in you differently. If you have yet to take any action at all, commit to crossing a line in the sand. You can do something small: buy LED lightbulbs, write to your elected representatives, vote for a climate-ready candidate. Do something today and tell someone what you did. These are simple steps, but the psychological leap is huge. In an instant, you will change something important about your identity and you will be on your way.

If, on the other hand, climate change is your profession and your life's work, try doing something new that puts your identity at risk again. Being one of the "good guys" can become its own comfort zone. It can make you complacent, and we still have work to do. Volunteering to help to organize and write an unsanctioned national strategic planning framework for public empowerment pushed me out of my own comfort zone, but I can already feel tremendous encouragement from this impressive community.

Take a risk. Draw a new line in the sand for yourself. Make sure it challenges your comfortable identity. Then cross it. This is what connects all of us in this crisis, no matter who we are. This is the foundation of our hope.

Author Biography

Tom Bowman is Strategic Advisor and Writing Team Lead for the U.S. Action for Climate Empowerment Strategic Planning Framework. The Framework is an initiative by social scientists, educators, scientists and activists to help the United States meet and exceed the goals of the Paris Agreement. Tom founded Bowman Design Group and Bowman Change, Inc., a strategic communication consultancy. He works with federal agencies, corporate leadership, entrepreneurs and leading cultural institutions such as NOAA, NASA, the National Academy of Sciences and the Aquarium of the Pacific. Tom's company received a Cool California Small Business of the Year Award for decarbonizing business operations. His work received White House Champions of Change recognition, and he was inducted into the International Green Industry Hall of Fame. Tom is a popular public speaker and author of *The Green Edge.*

Follow Tom Bowman at:
    www.BowmanChange.com
    www.facebook.com/Tom-Bowman-267568276686398
    @BowmanClimate

Appendix: Resources for Taking Action

If you are ready to take action for the first time or want to expand your range of activities, here are some resources to get you moving. As you engage and take new steps, remember that talking with others about your new connections and accomplishments will bolster your efforts and help create a wider culture that supports tackling the climate crisis.

Learn the Basics

If you would like to learn the fundamentals about the science of global warming, here are a few highly respected resources.

- *What We Know,* American Association for the Advancement of Science — https://whatweknow.aaas.org
- *Climate Change 101,* National Center for Science Education — https://ncse.ngo/climate-change-101
- *Climate Change 101,* Center for Climate and Energy Solutions — www.c2es.org/site/assets/uploads/2017/10/climate101-fullbook.pdf

Decarbonize Your Home and Workplace

There are three ways to approach reducing your carbon footprint. The simplest is to follow a step-by-step action guide. This approach will get you started with a minimum of effort. Since you will not be measuring your carbon emissions, the best way to track progress is by reductions in your monthly bills for electricity, natural gas, water and gasoline or diesel.

- *A Personal Action Guide to Becoming Climate Resilient,* written for a warm-weather region, but based on guiding principles that apply everywhere — www.aquariumofpacific.org/downloads/A_Personal_Action_Guide_to_Becoming_

Climate-Resilient.pdf
- *Cooler Smarter,* a book by the Union of Concerned Scientists
- *Zero Waste: The 80/20 Way,* a book by Stephanie Miller
- *Small business success stories* — https://coolcalifornia.arb. ca.gov/business-success-stories

The second approach is to estimate your carbon footprint based on average households or organizations that are similar to yours. Using this type of calculator takes a little more effort, but it will help you see where to focus your actions in order to get the biggest results. Several reputable carbon offset organizations provide simple online calculators. Here are two calculators that were developed by government agencies.

- *U.S. Environmental Protection Agency calculator* — www3. epa.gov/carbon-footprint-calculator/
- *Cool California,* a product of the California Air Resources Board, has calculators for households, small businesses, government agencies and schools — https://coolcalifornia. arb.ca.gov

The third and most detailed approach is to have your emissions measured and verified by a third party. The advantage is that the information will be much more precise, but there will be costs and much more legwork involved. Businesses, especially larger corporations, and governments tend to rely on third party measurement and verification by companies that offer this service. Here is a highly regarded nonprofit alternative.

- *The Climate Registry* — www.theclimateregistry.org

Join or Support a Climate Justice Organization
A quick online search will reveal many nonprofit organizations and networks that work on climate and environmental justice.

Consider supporting an organization in the town, city or rural area where you live. Here are a few nationwide organizations to consider as well.

- *Climate Justice Network* — www.climatejusticenetwork.org
- *National Association for the Advancement of Colored People (NAACP)* — www.naacp.org/environmental-climate-justice-about
- *Indigenous Environmental Network* — www.ienearth.org
- *Climate Justice Resilience Fund,* an international organization that funds community-led resilience solutions — www.cjrfund.org
- *U.S. National ACE Strategic Planning Framework* has a number of informative resources on its website — http://aceframework.us

Engage in Shared Learning or Activism

As with climate justice organizations, you can find a large number of organizations and networks online that approach the climate crisis from many different directions. Some organizations focus on legal action, others on political activism, while others build support for volunteer involvement in local neighborhoods and communities. Here are two of many large-scale movements.

- *Sunrise Movement,* a youth initiative for climate action — www.sunrisemovement.org
- *350.org,* a global movement for climate action — https://350.org

Business and Professional Action on Climate Change

The range of business networks, trade associations, and professional networks that provide advice and sustainability certifications is as diverse as the economy itself. Look within your industry and its trade associations and movements, and also within your state or local community where sustainability-minded businesses often form networks. Here are three nationwide examples that serve diverse industries and markets.

- *B Corporation Certification*—https://bcorporation.net
- *Green Business Network*—www.greenamerica.org
- *Sustainable Brands*—https://sustainablebrands.com

Climate Education

Educators working in K-12, community colleges, higher education and informal education share resources and promote climate curriculum through informal networks.

- *Climate Literacy and Energy Awareness Network (CLEAN)* is a U.S.-based network of climate educators—https://cleanet. org
- *Climate Education, Communication & Outreach Stakeholder Community (ClimateECOS)* is an international network of climate educators and communicators— https:// climateecos.org

Follow and Participate in the U.S. ACE National Strategic Planning Framework

The voluntary initiative described in chapter six tracks its progress online with recordings of inspiring panel discussions, the *Framework* report and a number of useful resources for public empowerment. If you work on climate solutions in any capacity, the opportunities for strategic collaboration that this project supports are meant for you. Take a look at the participating organizations. You can also help this initiative gain strength by bringing it to your elected representatives at the national, state and local levels. This is the pathway to establishing an official national strategy for the United States as part of the U.N. Framework Convention on Climate Change.

- *U.S. ACE National Strategic Planning Framework* — https:// aceframework.us

References

Chapter One: Are We Too Late to Solve the Climate Crisis?

1. Masson-Delmotte, V., Zhai, P., Pörtner, H.-O., Roberts, D., Skea, J., Shukla, P. R., Pirani, A., Moufouma-Okia, W., Péan, C., Pidcock, R., Connors, S., Matthews, J. B. R., Chen, Y., Zhou, X., Gomis, M. I., Lonnoy, E., Maycock, T., Tignor, M., Waterfield, T. (eds.) (2018) Summary for Policymakers, in *Global Warming of 1.5°C. An IPCC Special Report on the impacts of global warming of 1.5°C above pre-industrial levels and related global greenhouse gas emission pathways, in the context of strengthening the global response to the threat of climate change, sustainable development, and efforts to eradicate poverty* [Online], IPCC. Available at https://www.ipcc.ch/sr15/chapter/spm/ (Accessed 18 August 2020).

2. Leiserowitz, A., Maibach, E., Roser-Renouf, C., Rosenthal, S., Cutler, M., Kotcher, J. (2018) *Climate Change in the American Mind: March 2018* [Online], New Haven, Yale Program on Climate Change Communication. Available at https://climatecommunication.yale.edu/publications/climate-change-american-mind-march-2018/ (Accessed 18 August 2020).

3. Edelman (2019) *2019 Edelman Trust Barometer Global Report* [Online], Edelman. Available at https://www.edelman.com/sites/g/files/aatuss191/files/2019-02/2019_Edelman_Trust_Barometer_Global_Report.pdf (Accessed 18 August 2020).

4. Heath, C. and Heath, D. (2013) *Decisive*, New York, Crown Business, p. 3.

5. Gonzales, L. (2008) *Everyday Survival*, New York, W. W. Norton & Company, Inc., p. 48.

6. Gonzales (2008), p. 48.

7. Gonzales (2008), p. 28.

8. Gonzales (2008), p. 29.

9. Krosnick, J. A. (2007) Presentation to the Association of Science Technology Centers Annual Conference, Los Angeles, 13 October.

10. Oreskes, N. and Conway, E. M. (2010) *Merchants of Doubt*, New York, Bloomsbury Press.

11. Goldberg, M., Gustafson, A., Rosenthal, S., Kotcher, J., Maibach, E., Leiserowitz, A. (2020) *For the First Time, the Alarmed Are Now the Largest of Global Warming's Six Americas* [Online], New Haven, Yale Program on Climate Change Communication. Available at https://climatecommunication. yale.edu/publications/for-the-first-time-the-alarmed-are-now-the-largest-of-global-warmings-six-americas/ (Accessed 18 August 2020).

12. Leiserowitz, et al. (2018)

13. Bowman, T. (2016) *Toward Consensus on the Climate Communication Challenge: Report from a Dialogue of Researchers and Practitioners* [Online], Long Beach, Bowman Change, Inc. Available at http://bowmanchange.com (Accessed 18 August 2020).

Chapter Two: Hang the Climate Crisis Upside Down

1. Van der Liden, S. L., Leiserowitz, A., Feinberg, G. D., Maibach, E. (2014) How to communicate the scientific consensus on climate change: plain facts, pie charts or metaphors? *Climatic Change*, 6 July 2014 [Online]. DOI 10.1007/s10584-014-1190-4 (Accessed 1 May 2016).

2. Temple, J. (2018) 'Seaweed could make cows burb less methane and cut their carbon hoofprint', *MIT Technology Review*, 23 November [Online]. Available at https://www. technologyreview.com/2018/11/23/1826/how-seaweed-could-shrink-livestocks-global-carbon-hoofprint/ (Accessed 18 August 2020).

3. Masson-Delmotte, et al. (2018).

4. See Gonzales (2008) for an in-depth discussion of fast and slow mental processes and how they influence perceptions and behavior.
5. Gonzales (2008), p. 27.
6. Leiserowitz, et al. (2018).
7. Van der Liden, et al. (2014).
8. Semple, K. (2019) 'Central American farmers head to the U.S., fleeing climate change', *The New York Times* 13 April [Online]. Available at https://www.nytimes.com/2019/04/13/world/americas/coffee-climate-change-migration.html (Accessed 18 August 2020).
9. Manion, M., Zarakas, C., Wnuck, S., Haskell, J., Belova, A., Cooley, D., Dorn, J., Hoer, M., Mayo, L. (2017) *Analysis of the Public Health Impacts of the Regional Greenhouse Gas Initiative* [Online], Available at https://www.abtassociates.com/insights/publications/report/analysis-of-the-public-health-impacts-of-the-regional-greenhouse-gas (Accessed 18 August 2020).
10. McKenna, P. (2020) 'Elizabeth Warren on climate change: where the candidate stands', *Inside Climate News* 1 January [Online]. Available at https://insideclimatenews.org/news/25062019/elizabeth-warren-climate-change-global-warming-election-2020-candidate-profile (Accessed 18 August 2020).
11. Bowman, T. (2014) 'How can we accelerate carbon reductions (with Jon Koomey)?', *Climate Report* [Podcast]. 28 June. Available at http://bowmanchange.com/posts/category/climate-report/ (Accessed 18 August 2020).
12. Bowman (2014).
13. Edmonds (2012) 2012 Tesla Model S review, *Edmunds Expert Review* [Online]. Available at https://www.edmunds.com/tesla/model-s/2012/review/ (Accessed 18 August 2020).
14. Bowman, T. (2014).
15. Maibach, M., Myers, T., Leiserowitz, A. (2014) Climate

scientists need to set the record straight: there is a scientific consensus that human-caused climate change is happening, *Advancing Earth and Space Science* 4 April 2014 [Online]. Available at https://agupubs.onlinelibrary.wiley.com/doi/full/10.1002/2013EF000226 (Accessed 18 August 2020).

16. Esty, D. and Winston, A. (2006) *Green to Gold*, New Haven, Yale University Press, p. 209.

17. Verified emissions reports from all Climate Registry members are available for public review. See https://www.theclimateregistry.org.

18. California Air Resources Board (2009) 'Sustainable by Design', *CoolCalifornia.org* [Online]. Available at https://coolcalifornia.arb.ca.gov/story/bowman-design-group (Accessed 18 August 2020).

19. Bowman, T. (2014) 'Can brand promotion drive social change (with Denise Taschereau)?', *Climate Report* [Podcast]. 16 August. Available at http://bowmanchange.com/posts/category/climate-report/ (Accessed 18 August 2020).

20. Le Quéré, C., Jackson, R. B., Jones, M. W., Smith, A. J. P., Abernathy, S., Andrew, R. M., De-Gol, A. J., Willis, D. R., Shan, Y., Canadell, J. G., Friedlingstein, P., Creutzig, F., Peters, G. P. (2020) Temporary reduction in daily global CO_2 emissions during the COVID-19 forced confinement, *Nature Climate Change* vol. 10, July 2020, pp 647-653 [Online]. Available at https://www.nature.com/articles/s41558-020-0797-x (Accessed 18 August 2020).

21. Koetsier, J. (2020) '6 reasons most want to work from home even after coronavirus', *Forbes* 13 June [Online]. Available at https://www.forbes.com/sites/johnkoetsier/2020/06/13/6-reasons-most-want-to-work-from-home-even-after-coronavirus/#1437ce8938fa (Accessed 18 August 2020).

22. Stoknes, P. E. and Bowman, T. (2017) 'Trump's pro-coal orders are doomed to fail', *Time,* 29 March [Online]. Available at https://time.com/4709796/trump-epa-climate-

fossil-fuels/?xid=homepage (Accessed 18 August 2020).

23. Reuters (2017) 'World Bank to cease financing upstream oil and gas after 2019', *Reuters* 12 December [Online]. Available at https://www.reuters.com/article/us-climatechange-summit-worldbank/world-bank-to-cease-financing-upstream-oil-and-gas-after-2019-idUSKBN1E61LE (Accessed 18 August 2020).

24. Gronewold, N. (2019) 'Development bank stops giving loans for fossil fuel projects', *Climate Wire* 15 November [Online]. Available at https://www.eenews.net/stories/1061552241 (Accessed 18 August 2020).

25. Wikipedia (2020) *Greensburg, Kansas* [Online], 24 July 2020. Available at https://en.wikipedia.org/wiki/Greensburg,_Kansas (Accessed 18, August 2020).

26. American Wind Energy Association (2019) *Wind Energy in Iowa* [Online]. Available at https://www.awea.org/Awea/media/Resources/StateFactSheets/Iowa.pdf (Accessed 18 August 2020).

Chapter Three: A View from the Front Lines

1. U.S. Bureau of Labor Statistics (2020) *TED: The Economics Daily* [Online]. Available at https://www.bls.gov/opub/ted/2019/unemployment-rate-unchanged-at-3-point-6-percent-in-may-2019.htm?view_full (Accessed 18 August 2020).

2. Fischhoff, B. (2007) Nonpersuasive communication about matters of greatest urgency: climate change, *Environmental Science & Technology,* vol. 41, no. 21, pp. 7204-7208 [Online]. Available at https://pubs.acs.org/doi/10.1021/es0726411# (Accessed 18 August 2020), p. 7206.

3. Hoffman, A. J. (2015) *How Culture Shapes the Climate Change Debate,* Stanford, Stanford Briefs, p. 4.

4. Bowman (2016).

5. Fischhoff (2007), p. 7206.

6. Carr, S. (2020) 'How many ads do we see a day in 2020?', *PPC Project,* 9 April [Blog]. Available at https://ppcprotect. com/how-many-ads-do-we-see-a-day/ (Accessed 18 August 2020).

7. Science News (2013) 'Big data, for better or worse: 90% of world's data generated over last two years', *Science Daily,* 22 May [Online]. Available at https://www.sciencedaily.com/ releases/2013/05/130522085217.htm (Accessed 18 August 2020).

Chapter Four: What Helps People Engage?

1. Goldberg, et al. (2020)

2. Leiserowitz, et al. (2018).

3. Leiserowitz, A., Maibach, E., Rosenthal, S., Kotcher, J., Ballew, M., Bergquist, P., Gustafson, A., Goldberg, M., Wang, X. (2020) *Politics & Global Warming, April 2020* [Online], New Haven, Yale Program on Climate Change Communication. Available at https://climatecommunication.yale.edu/ publications/politics-global-warming-april-2020/ (Accessed 18 August 2020).

4. Molina, M., McCarthy, J., Wall, D., Alley, R., Cobb, K., Cole, J., Das, S., Diffenbaugh, N., Emanuel, K., Frumkin, H., Hayhoe, K., Parmesan, C., Shepherd, M. (2014) *What We Know: The Reality, Risks and Response to Climate Change* [Online], Washington, American Association for the Advancement of Science. Available at https://whatweknow.aaas.org/get-the-facts/ (Accessed 18 August 2020).

5. Climate Health Action (2019) *U.S. Call to Action on Climate, Health, and Equity: A Policy Action Agenda* [Online], Available at https://climatehealthaction.org/cta/climate-health-equity-policy/ (Accessed 18 August 2020).

6. Hultman, N., Frisch, C., Clark, L., Kennedy, K., Bodnar, P., Hansel, P., Cyrus, T., Manion, M., Edwards, M., Lund, J., Bowman, C., Jaeger, J., Cui, R., Clapper, A., Sen, A., Sha,

D., Westphal, M., Jaglom, W., Altamirano, J.C., Hashimoto, H., Dennis, M., Hammound, K., Henderson, C., Zwicker, G., Ryan, M., O'Neill, J., Goldfield, E. (2019) *Accelerating America's Climate Pledge: Going All In to Build a Prosperous, Low-Carbon Economy for the United States* [Online], New York, NY: Bloomberg Philanthropies. Available at https://www.americaspledgeonclimate.com/accelerating-americas-pledge-2/ (Accessed 18 August 2020).

7. Bowman (2016), p. 12.
8. Bowman (2016), p. 12.
9. Bowman (2016), p. 12.
10. Gould, R. (2011) What does it take to market social and behavioral change? paper presented at *Carbon Smarts Conference*. Lowell, 20 October.
11. Krosnick, J. A. (2010) 'The climate majority', *The New York Times* 8 June [Online]. Available at https://www.nytimes.com/2010/06/09/opinion/09krosnick.html?pagewanted=2&th&emc=th (Accessed 18 August 2020).
12. Sachs, J (2012) *Winning the Story Wars,* Boston, Harvard Business Review Press.
13. Gould (2011).
14. Small Business & Entrepreneurship Council (2018) *Facts & Data on Small Business and Entrepreneurship* [Online]. Available at https://sbecouncil.org/about-us/facts-and-data/ (Accessed 18 August 2020).
15. Erickson, G. and Lorentzen, L. (2004) *Raising the Bar,* San Francisco, Jossey-Bass, p. 23.
16. Erickson, G. and Lorentzen, L. (2004), p. 32.
17. Fischhoff (2007) p. 7206.
18. Gould (2011).
19. RepublicEn (n.d.) *Solving Climate Change* [Online]. Available at https://republicen.org (Accessed 18 August 20).
20. Heath, C. and Heath, D. (2010) *Switch,* New York, Broadway

Books.

21. Gonzales, L. (2003) *Deep Survival,* New York, W. W. Norton & Company.

22. Bowman (2016).

23. Bowman (2016), p. 14.

24. Leiserowitz, et al. (2018).

25. Gould (2011).

26. Gould (2011).

Chapter Five: Climate Justice and a White Male

1. Worland, J. (2019) 'Climate change has already increased global inequity. It will only get worse', *Time* 22 April [Online]. Available at https://time.com/5575523/climate-change-inequality/ (Accessed 18 August 2020).

2. Kendi, I. X. (2020) 'What the racial data show', *The Atlantic* 6 April [Online]. Available at https://www.theatlantic.com/ideas/archive/2020/04/coronavirus-exposing-our-racial-divides/609526/ (Accessed 18 August 2020).

3. Parker, K., Horowitz, J. M., Anderson, M. (2020) 'Amid protests, majorities across racial and ethnic groups express support for the Black Lives Matter Movement', *Pew Research Center* 12 June [Online]. Available at https://www.pewsocialtrends.org/2020/06/12/amid-protests-majorities-across-racial-and-ethnic-groups-express-support-for-the-black-lives-matter-movement/ (Accessed 18 August 2020).

4. Select Committee on the Climate Crisis (2020) *Solving the Climate Crisis.* Washington, United States House of Representatives.

5. Kaplan, S. (2020) 'How America's hottest city will survive climate change', *The Washington Post* 8 July [Online]. Available at https://www.washingtonpost.com/graphics/2020/climate-solutions/phoenix-climate-change-heat/?no_nav=true&tid=a_classic-iphone&p9w22b2p=b2p22p9w00098 (Accessed 18 August

2020).

6. Mann, M. E. (2012) *The Hockey Stick and the Climate Wars*, New York, Columbia University Press.

7. Bowman (2016).

8. E360 Digest (2009) 'NASA's James Hansen arrested during coal mining protest'. *Yale Environment 360* 24 June [Online]. Available at https://e360.yale.edu/digest/nasas-james-hansen-arrested-during-coal-mining-protest (Accessed 18 August 2020).

9. Bowman, T. (2013) 'Have climate reports been too cautious (with Naomi Oreskes and Richard Somerville)?' *Climate Report* [Podcast]. 16 February. Available at http://bowmanchange.com/posts/category/climate-report/page/3/ (Accessed 18 August 2020).

10. Bharara, P. (2020) 'Awakening to American truths (with Cory Booker)', *Stay Tuned with Preet* [Podcast]. 16 July. Available at https://cafe.com/stay-tuned-podcast/ (Accessed 18 August 2020).

11. Baldwin, J. (2010) *The Cross of Redemption: Uncollected Writings,* New York, Pantheon Books, p. 73.

12. Gonzales (2008), p. 46.

Chapter Six: A Plan to Turn Things Around

1. Bowman (2016), p. 9.

2. Rowell, A. (2020) 'Chevron hires PR company to paint Green New Deal as "racist" while claiming to support BLM protests', *Oil Change International* 22 June [Online]. Available at http://priceofoil.org/2020/06/22/chevron-hires-pr-company-to-paint-green-new-deal-as-racist-while-claiming-to-support-blm-protests/ (Accessed 18 August 2020).

3. Paas, L. and Goodman, D. (2016). *Action for Climate Empowerment: Guidelines for Accelerating Solutions through Education, Training and Public Awareness.* Paris and Bonn, United Nations Educational, Scientific and Cultural

Organization and the Secretariat of the United Nations Convention on Climate Change, p. 2.

4. United Nations (2012) Doha work programme on Article 6 of the convention, *United Nations Framework Convention on Climate Change* [Online]. Available at https://unfccc.int/resource/docs/2012/sbi/eng/l47.pdf (Accessed 18 August 2020).

5. Fischhoff (2007), p. 7206.

6. Fischhoff, B. (2016) 'Fischhoff in the Huffington Post: Climate Talk', *Carnegie Mellon University* 25 July [Online]. Available at https://www.cmu.edu/epp/news/2016/climate-talk.html (Accessed 18 August 2020).

7. Yankelovich, D. (1999) *The Magic of Dialogue,* New York, Touchstone, p. 17.

8. United Nations Education Sector (2020) *Integrating Action for Climate Empowerment into Nationally Determined Contributions,* Paris, United Nations Educational, Scientific and Cultural Organization, p. 4.

9. Pass, L, and Goodman, D. (2016), p. 6.

10. United Nations Education Sector (2020), p. 4.

11. United Nations Education Sector (2020), p. 4.

12. United Nations Education Sector (2020), p. 4.

13. United Nations Education Sector (2020), p. 4.

14. United Nations Climate Change (2018) *2018 Talanoa Dialogue Platform* [Online]. Available at https://unfccc.int/process-and-meetings/the-paris-agreement/the-paris-agreement/2018-talanoa-dialogue-platform (Accessed 18 August 2020).

15. United States Action for Climate Empowerment Strategic Planning Framework (2020) [Online]. Available at https://aceframework.us (Accessed 18 August 2020).

16. Plumer, B. (2013) 'Why do Californians use less electricity than everyone else?', *The Washington Post* 12 August [Online]. Available at https://www.washingtonpost.com/news/wonk/

wp/2013/08/12/why-do-californians-use-less-electricity-than-everyone-else/ (Accessed 18 August 2020).

17. Who Is In? (n.d.) *We Are Still In* [Online]. Available at https://www.wearestillin.com/signatories (Accessed 18 August 2020).

18. Pass, L, and Goodman, D. (2016), p. 2.

Chapter Seven: Luckily, It Comes Down to Us

1. Gonzales, L. (2012) *Surviving Survival*, New York, W. W. Norton & Company, p. 205.

2. Gonzales, L. (2012), p. 209.

CHANGEMAKERS
BOOKS

TRANSFORMATION

Transform your life, transform your world – Changemakers
Books publishes for individuals committed to transforming
their lives and transforming the world. Our readers seek to
become
positive, powerful agents of change. Changemakers Books
inform, inspire, and provide practical wisdom and skills to
empower us to write the next chapter of humanity's future.
www.changemakers-books.com

The *Resilience* Series

The Resilience Series is a collaborative effort by the authors of Changemakers Books in response to the 2020 coronavirus epidemic. Each concise volume offers expert advice and practical exercises for mastering specific skills and abilities. Our intention is that by strengthening your resilience, you can better survive and even thrive in a time of crisis.
www.resilience-books.com

Adapt and Plan for the New Abnormal - in the COVID-19 Coronavirus Pandemic
Gleb Tsipursky

Aging with Vision, Hope and Courage in a Time of Crisis
John C. Robinson

Connecting With Nature in a Time of Crisis
Melanie Choukas-Bradley

Going Within in a Time of Crisis
P. T. Mistlberger

Grow Stronger in a Time of Crisis
Linda Ferguson

Handling Anxiety in a Time of Crisis
George Hoffman

Navigating Loss in a Time of Crisis
Jules De Vitto

The Life-Saving Skill of Story
Michelle Auerbach

Virtual Teams - Holding the Center When You Can't Meet Face-to-Face
Carlos Valdes-Dapena

Virtually Speaking - Communicating at a Distance
Tim Ward and Teresa Erickson

Current Bestsellers from Changemakers Books

Pro Truth
A Practical Plan for Putting Truth Back into Politics
Gleb Tsipursky and Tim Ward

How can we turn back the tide of post-truth politics, fake news, and misinformation that is damaging our democracy? In the lead up to the 2020 US Presidential Election, Pro Truth provides the answers.

An Antidote to Violence
Evaluating the Evidence
Barry Spivack and Patricia Anne Saunders

It's widely accepted that Transcendental Meditation can create peace for the individual, but can it create peace in society as a whole? And if it can, what could possibly be the mechanism?

Finding Solace at Theodore Roosevelt Island
Melanie Choukas-Bradley

A woman seeks solace on an urban island paradise in Washington D.C. through 2016-17, and the shock of the Trump election.

the bottom
a theopoetic of the streets
Charles Lattimore Howard

An exploration of homelessness fusing theology, jazz-verse and intimate storytelling into a challenging, raw and beautiful tale.

The Soul of Activism
A Spirituality for Social Change
Shmuly Yanklowitz

A unique examination of the power of interfaith spirituality to fuel the fires of progressive activism.

Future Consciousness
The Path to Purposeful Evolution
Thomas Lombardo

An empowering evolutionary vision of wisdom and the human mind to guide us in creating a positive future.

Preparing for a World that Doesn't Exist - Yet
Rick Smyre and Neil Richardson

This book is about an emerging Second Enlightenment and the capacities you will need to achieve success in this new, fast-evolving world.